Love, Laughter, & Life

BY SUSAN BARLOW

DEDICATION

To all my posterity. I hope you learn (and laugh) from my experiences that shaped who I have become.

TABLE OF CONTENTS

We added the original audio files to Brent's blog in case you want to listen to the original recordings:
https://brentabarlow.blogspot.com/p/audio-files.html

CHAPTER 1: BIRTH AND ADOPTION

My Birth Parents (Audio Vol. 11)

I want to start off by talking a little about my birth parents. I consider my parents to be the ones who raised me because that's more important than the ones responsible for giving me life. It's interesting to know about my physical and mental health and the heritage I got from my birth parents. Colleen Wooldridge, my birth mother, was a 16-year-old Caucasian from Coos Bay, Oregon. My birth father, also from Coos Bay, Oregon, was Chinese. His grandfather Gow Why had immigrated to San Francisco by way of steamship from mainland China where he had left his wife and daughter of two years with his parents. He had taken out a loan for his passage and was expected to pay back the loan as soon as he found work. Gow worked many jobs and eventually opened a grocery store. He eventually married a girl from San Francisco, and she helped him with the grocery store. They had several children together – the oldest was named Bert. Bert grew up in Marshfield, which was later named Coos Bay, where he went to school and eventually married Bessie. Bert and Bessie had a large family, and their oldest child was named Harry Why. Harry, my birth father, was raised in Coos Bay where he attended public school. In high school, Harry met my birth mother Colleen Woolridge.

During high school, Harry went back to China for one year, which put him a year behind in his studies. Colleen and Harry met at school and started dating. You have to remember that back then, mixed relationships were not a thing people looked in favor upon. And so, there was a lot of discrimination from parents and from other students. Because of this, they dated in secret. Colleen's father eventually found out about it. He was a military man and not pleased at all with the situation. He requested a transfer, and the family moved from Coos Bay to Fort Ord, California. It's uncertain whether or not Harry finished school or quit early, but he joined the Air Force and went to Texas. In Texas, he met a girl that he would eventually marry. One theory is that Harry never knew Colleen was pregnant when she left Coos Bay with her parents. They probably never saw each other again.

Karen, Brent's sister and my sister-in-law, said she did some research and found out that when Colleen was pregnant, she worked in the canneries in San Francisco. There are some papers stating she worked there until it was time to have the baby. She stayed with her aunt in Paso Robles, California, which is where I was born. I was born in the county hospital in Paso Robles. Paso Robles is about 30 miles north of San Luis Obispo. It's over

My mom Alice & dad Cecil as newlyweds

the grade, as we called it, because you have to go over a mountain to get to Paso Robles from San Luis Obispo.

When I was born, neither family wanted to keep me. Colleen was a young girl, barely 16, who didn't want to see me when I was born. I think the reason for that was if she saw her baby, she knew it would be harder to give it up. She realized she had no way of taking care of me, so she agreed to put me up for adoption. I'm not sure if Harry was ever even contacted or if he knew about the pregnancy at all. There is no indication they even kept in contact after leaving Oregon. Harry married Ruth in Texas, and they eventually had six children. They lived their married life in Coos Bay where Harry became very prominent and wealthy in the community. He was well-known for his work at the University in Coos Bay and was a contributor to many different organizations. Harry died living in Coos Bay when he was in his late 90's. Colleen had a different story. She married three times and died of lung cancer when she was 63. She had been a chain smoker throughout her life. When she died, she was living in Bentonville, Oregon with her third husband and two daughters from a former marriage. Her daughters are still living in Oregon today.

My Adoption (Audio Vol. 10)

Now, I'm going to talk a little about my background because the parents I consider my real parents were not the parents I was born to. I was born in Paso Robles, California and became a ward of the court. There was a law in California at the time stating a bi-racial baby had to be adopted by bi-racial parents. As there did not seem to be anyone who met these criteria interested in the adoption, I remained in the County Hospital in Paso Robles for several weeks before I went into the foster care system. It was at that point I went to live with Alice and Cecil Day. Alice and Cecil had been married for a few years and were unable to have children of their own. Since they wanted children so desperately, they decided to take in foster children until they could have their own. And thus, the miracle of my life began.

My adoptive parents were a lot older than most parents who had children around my age at the time. Let me tell you a little about my mom. Alice Elizabeth Jacklin was only 21 when her mom and dad were in an automobile accident, coming home from the Salt Lake Temple. A truck broad-sided them when swerving into the wrong lane. It was a major accident. My grandma died on the way to the hospital, and my grandpa was critically injured and spent some time in the hospital before coming home. He still was unable to do much, so my mother, who was one of the oldest children at home, took over. They had 11 children in total, so she had 10 siblings, and her two older siblings were a brother who was on a mission and a sister who was going to college.

She would help with outdoor tasks along with taking care of the home and her younger siblings. They had a big farm with a large garden to tend to, hay to bale, and animals to care for. My grandpa relied on my mom a lot as it took quite a while for my grandpa to get back on his feet. My mom spent most of her younger years helping out with household responsibilities.

She met my father through some good friends she had grown up with who were on a mission from American Fork to California. These friends would write letters to my mother while on their missions, and one day, they met this recent convert. They got him and my mom writing letters back and forth, and the two got to know each other that way before they ever became romantically involved.

Eventually, my grandfather (on my dad Cecil's side) had found out that Alice had a background in medicine. She worked for a well-known doctor in American Fork and would help deliver babies. When Cecil's mother became terminally ill with cancer, my grandpa wrote to my mother and asked if he could hire her to come to California and take care of his wife in the latter stages of her life. She agreed, and so, she went down to California and lived with my grandpa, grandma, and her future husband Cecil. She stayed there and took care of Cecil's mom until she passed away, and during that time, she got to know

Cecil with his Parents (Warren Claire Day) & (Lillian Garren Day)

my grandma really well. My mom and my dad would talk with her a lot as well. After my grandma died, my mom went back to American Fork, but Cecil continued writing to her.

As a side note, my dad had joined the church a few years earlier, and my grandma was very interested in it. My dad had talked to her a lot about it, and she wanted to hear more about the church. She wanted the missionaries to come and give her the lessons, but my grandpa was very adamant about not doing that. He had some issues with the church, and he didn't like his son being a member. He could see that his son and my mom were becoming interested in each other early on, and when they decided to get married, he was very against it. Before my grandma died, she never got to know a lot about the church, but she knew she wanted to know more, and she knew that she possibly wanted to be baptized, but grandpa would not have it. But, my dad had at least introduced her to the gospel and this kind of gave her an opportunity to know in the next life that she wanted to find out more, which was a good place.

Before long, my dad was visiting my mom in American Fork regularly. Eventually, he went to Utah to get married in the Salt Lake Temple. My grandpa was very upset because he was not a member of the church, so he could not go into the temple to witness the wedding. That drove another thorn into his side and made him even more upset. But, the story continues. As for my mom and dad, they didn't have much money, so my grandpa offered to let them live with him because he needed some care as well. So, my mom and dad went to live with my grandpa in San Luis Obispo after their honeymoon in San Francisco. My mom took care of him. She cut his hair every week, prepared his meals, and did his washing. He was a very proud man, so he would leave her 50 cents under her plate every Friday night to pay for all the work she did for him. Three or four years went by, and they wanted to have a family. My mom especially wanted a large family because she came from a large family, but they couldn't seem to get pregnant. They went to doctors and had some tests run and found out they were unable to have children. My mom always loved children – she raised her brothers and sisters, even the youngest who was a baby at the time – and so, they decided to take care of foster children.

This is how I came into their home. When I was born, California had a law stating you had to be adopted by parents of the same ethnicity as you. In other words, since I was Chinese and Caucasian, I had to be adopted by parents that were Chinese and

My mom & dad on their wedding day

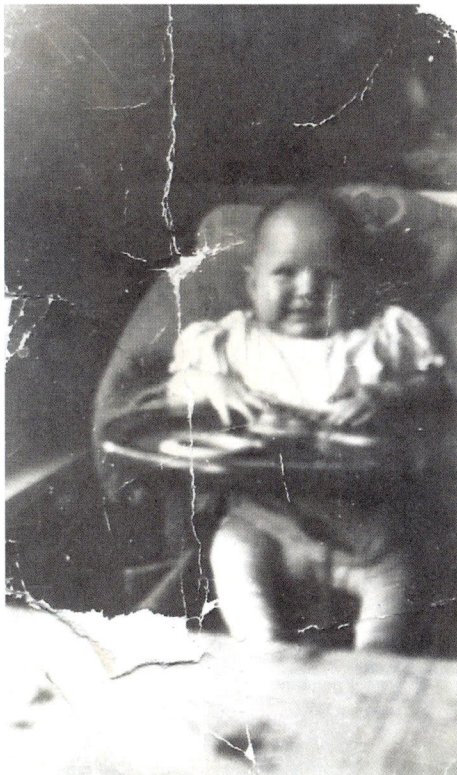

Sue as a Baby

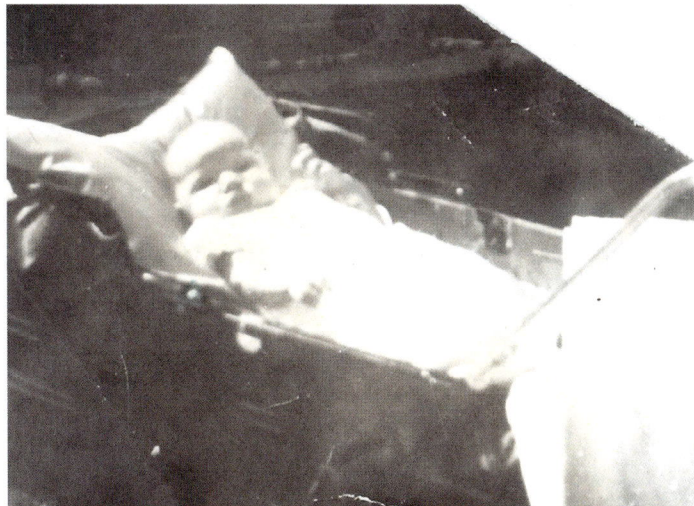

Sue about 1-2 months old

Caucasian which was very difficult to find. I was not adopted, so I became a ward of the court and was put into foster care. When my parents decided to take in foster children, I was one of the first ones they took in, and I was a baby. I had been in the hospital for several weeks before I went into foster care. At about three weeks old, I went into their home. They raised me and they loved me and decided they wanted to keep me as their own child. It took about two years for adoption proceedings to be concluded. But the problem was with this law, it was hard to adopt a person of a different combination of races, so they had to go to court to get special permission to adopt me since I was a different combination of races than they were.

At the time, the ward my parents were members of had a stake president who knew a lot about the law. He was also a very dear friend of ours. He went to court with my mom and dad, and he testified regarding their character, about what they had done in the church, and how they were upstanding citizens that contributed to the community . Because of his good standing with the community, the adoption was granted. And that's how I became a member of their family.

One side note – there was a letter from a social worker who felt it was a mistake, me being adopted

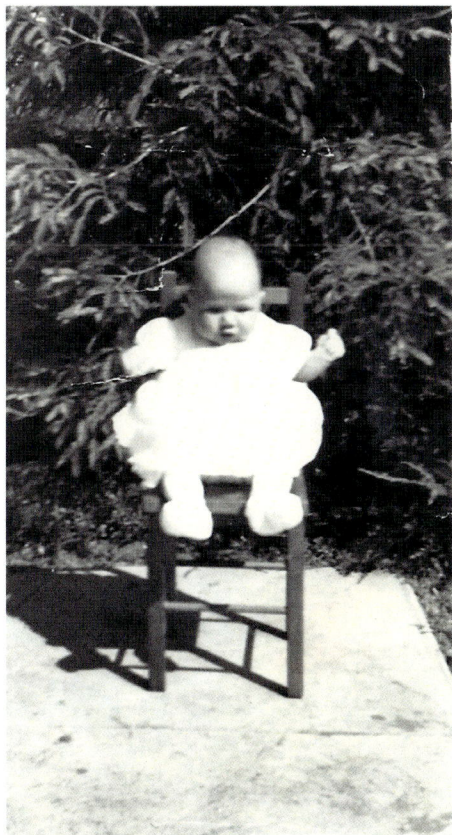

Me sitting up by the pine tree

into a family who were members of some strange church. She thought it was terrible that I would be raised in THAT church, but It turned out to be such a blessing! It was kind of a miracle of how I came into the church because if I hadn't been adopted into their family, who knows where I would have been. I feel that It was the Lord intervening in my life to give me a family who would raise me in the church. Both of my parents were very strong in their faith and had strong testimonies. I got the full program of the church as I was growing up and developed a testimony through them. What a blessing it was indeed!

CHAPTER 2: MY PARENTS AND GRANDPARENTS

Memories of My Grandparents

By the time I was adopted, both of my grandmas had already passed away. My Grandma Day (Lillian Cordelia Garren Day) died from complications after a stroke she had had when coming home from visiting my Aunt Gertrude and Uncle Harry in Oxnard. She never fully recovered but instead became progressively more ill. My dad and grandpa had a difficult time taking care of all her needs. As I said before, my mom was hired to care for her during the last month of her life. By the time my mom had made arrangements to come to San Luis Obispo, my grandma's health had gotten worse. My mom was able to spend a month with my grandma before she died on August 2, 1939.

My other grandma, Martha O'Neal Jacklin, died when she was coming home from the Salt Lake Temple with my grandpa, and a truck hit their car. My grandpa was critically injured, and my grandma died in the ambulance on the way to the hospital.

At the time of my adoption, I had two grandpas. My

Sue age 1 with my Mom

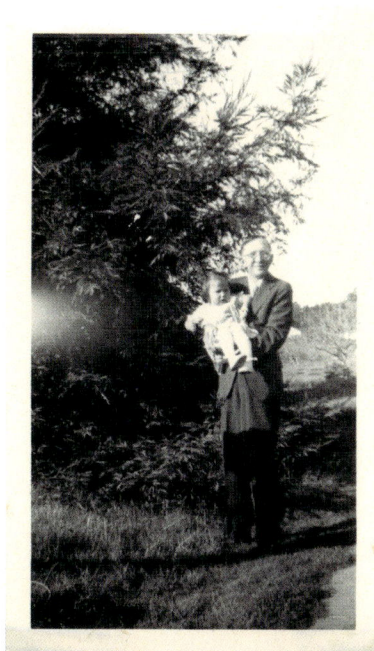

Sue age 1 with my Dad

Portrait of me in my new crocheted dress

Grandma Day (Lillian Cordeila Garren Day)

Grandpa Day (postal carrier) in Fiesta Day Parade

My Grandpa & Grandma Jacklin (John & Martha Jacklin)

Grandpa Day & Sue (age 9 months)

The pitcher I used to collect well water with Grandpa Jacklin

dad's father was named Warren Claire Day. He was born in Woodbury County, Iowa on May 1, 1877. When my dad was born, my grandpa was an assistant miller in Paso Robles, California, working for the Sperry Flour Company. He also worked as a cook and a waiter at the Paso Robles Hotel. He later worked as a letter carrier for the U.S. Postal Service. My dad eventually worked for the U.S. Postal Service for a while as well.

My Grandpa Jacklin lived in American Fork, Utah. Each year, we would go to Utah to visit our Jacklin relatives, which were many since my mom came from a large family (10 siblings in total). My mom was like a mother to many of her younger siblings growing up since their mom was killed in the accident.

One of my favorite memories of my Grandpa Jacklin was going to the well in his backyard to get cold, fresh well water. I had my own special pitcher that I used to get the water.

Alice and Sue's Patriarchal Blessings (Audio Vol. 16)

Now, I want to talk a little about patriarchal blessings. I'll start with my mom's patriarchal blessing. She got it when she was somewhere between 18 and 20 years old, but in her patriarchal blessing, it said that she would be older when she became a mother. It relates to "as Sarah of old she would have a child." She was always so emotional about me when she would think about this because she felt that "it was meant to be... that I was to come to their family because of her patriarchal blessing."

She was 42 when I was adopted, so she always looked at me as, in reality, a gift from God. She always put so much faith in me. She believed that I was such a good person and trusted me completely. I wasn't really that good – I was okay but not super good as a child. I didn't have a curfew. She gave me lots of responsibilities and always expected me to make the right decision. In doing so, I'd sometimes get into situations that were awkward. For instance, I was on a date once, and the guy tried to talk me into staying out later, I would make up a

Grandpa Jacklin & Sue at Grandpa's house in American Fork

lie and say, "Oh I have a curfew, and I have to be home by 11:30." I never told my mom or dad, but I always got in on time because I would make up this story. I did this because my mother put so much faith in me that I knew I couldn't let her down.

When I was 16 or 17, I decided I wanted to get a patriarchal blessing. Our stake headquarters where our patriarch lived was in Santa Maria about 30 miles south of San Luis Obispo. My friend Lynne Greenall was a year younger than I was. We were always good friends. We were even roommates at BYU for a while. Anyway, she and I drove down to Santa Maria after we'd fasted the day before. We drove to the patriarch's house, and he took us one at a time to talk to us about patriarchal blessings. I remember questioning how he could get this inspiration from our Father in Heaven about me personally. As I said, I had some things in my life that I was wondering about, so I was looking to my patriarchal blessing for some answers to these questions.

Grandpa Jacklin with Sue and cousin Bobby Jean Gooch

The first part of my patriarchal blessing says the circumstances surrounding my birth were not important, rather it was important that I was raised by people of good faith who had my best interest at heart. It was meant to be for me to join the family I did and answer their

Grandma Alice and our kids

prayers. I always thought it was strange how we ended up together, being that they were not Chinese at all, they were older, and they weren't the typical young family looking to adopt. And so, through my teenage years, I always wondered about this. My patriarchal blessing clarified that.

My blessing also says I would minister to the needs of those who suffer. So, I always thought I would be a nurse. I started at BYU in the nursing program, but I realized I didn't think I could handle part of nursing. I ended up changing my major to teaching, which I dearly loved. So, sometimes patriarchal blessings are not translated easily or in the way you think they should be, but you find out it really fits the way your life turns out. I still take care of people through my relief society callings and by just helping others. So really, that part of it was true, but it's interesting it wasn't my main career like I thought it was.

According to my patriarchal blessing in regards to getting married and having a family, it states that I would be sorely tried in choosing a mate. It stresses how important it is to marry in the temple because in doing this I would be able to do what the Lord expects me to do. It also states that I would be blessed with a good and noble posterity. I would have children born to me who were choices and who were good children, and my greatest responsibility in life was to be a good wife and mother. My favorite part is that I will have the opportunity and the power to weld my family into a unit that will love one another. Patriarchal blessings are such great guidelines to have in life, because reading them over and over helps you stay on the right path.

Grandma Alice and Her Grandkids (Audio Vol. 20)

Now, I'd like to talk a little about my mom; taking care of her as she got older, the adjustment after my dad passed away, and the move back up to American Fork. My mom lived in a little one-bedroom house she was renting. It was our job to make sure she always had what she needed and was ok where she lived, But she was a very independent lady. She had a lot of health problems, especially with arthritis, but she was sharp as a tack, mentally. She could clearly remember details from my life when I was little, when I was married and the births of our children. So, she was still with it mentally, but it was getting harder for her to do things around her house towards the end of her life.

We used to drive to American Fork to go over to her house at least once a week, usually more than that. We would take her shopping so she could go and get the food that she needed. I usually took Brian, Kristin, Jon, and the little ones. It was kind of a fun thing for the kids because when she would go grocery shopping, she'd let the kids pick out their favorite snacks. Brian would

Grandma and her first grandchild Doug

say, "Grandma, you know, I really loved that wrestling magazine that you got me." And despite my objections, she would always give in and buy them more stuff. So, that was always a great experience for my kids because they always had fun with Grandma.

We would always stop at the park in the middle of American Fork. There was a drinking fountain at the corner of the park, and my kids thought for sure that it was the

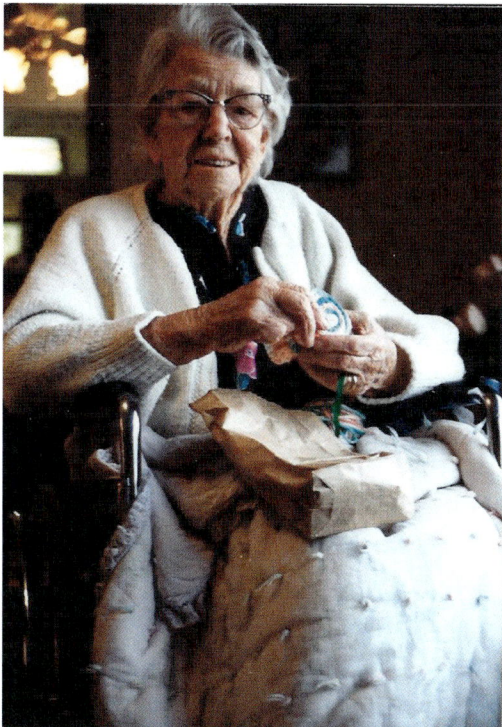

Grandma Alice Day

best water ever, and they would be healthy because they drank it. They always called it "healthy water".

Another thing I remember about Grandma's house is my mother had a wood fireplace which would always need a fresh stack of wood. No matter the time of year, she would always have at least one fire early in the morning. One time, I remember Kristen and Doug were going out to get the wood. It was in a shed in the backyard of her house, and they would pile all the wood up in the wagon, bring it to the front door, and take turns carrying the wood into her house. And on this day, it was very cold, so we knew we had to get her wood because she was running low. So, they went out to get it, and Kristen was trying to push the wagon from the back when she slid on the ice. She hit her mouth on the edge of the wagon and broke off her front tooth. It did not break off evenly; It broke off in a jagged piece so we called her dentist who met us at the dentist office on the way home, and he put a cap on it. It looked all right but there was quite a bit of trauma that day.

One other thing I remember is mowing her lawns in the summertime. She would always want to be involved, so she would sit in her chair and hold the bags open for the kids to dump the grass in. Her grass would always be so tall and thick that the bag on the back of the lawn mower would need to be emptied several times during the process.

My mother would always have a bottle of orange vitamin C shaped like an orange at the bottom of her purse. Anytime we'd see her, she'd say, "Okay guys, you gotta have some vitamin C." And so, she'd give everybody one . She'd also have random candies at the bottom of her purse, and the kids would always say, "Grandma do you have any candy?" and she would dig out these pieces that were probably filled with dirt. They'd have to brush them off to eat them.

My mom was such an interesting lady. She would always crochet all sorts of things for the grandkids, neighbor's kids, her friend's kids and anyone else she could think of. She would make little tiny socks that they could hang on the Christmas tree and put candy canes in them. Another thing she was known for was her crocheted jack-o-lanterns that she filled with candy. She was also famous for her afghans which she made for each one of her grandkids as well as a beautiful bedspread and tablecloth she made for me.

My mother was also a caregiver for Brandon. When I had to go back to work in the mornings, she volunteered to watch Brandon who had casts on his legs and was only 2-3 months old. She was in good health and felt she could be a good help to me, which she was. Besides the point of taking excellent care of him, she spoiled him rotten. She rocked him, sang him to sleep, and read him stories. Brandon probably got a lot better care than I could ever have given him at the time.

Alice's Last Chapter (Audio Vol. 43)

My mother and I were always very close. She often told me how blessed she was because I came into her life. She would say that even if she had physically given birth to me, she could never pick a better daughter to have. So, with my mother telling me all the time how great and wonderful I was and how much she loved me, I knew she totally loved me.

The story I'm going to tell is when she was dying. She was living in a nursing home at the time. The doctor changed her medication on a certain day, and she was sitting by herself in a room at the TV. After they moved her there, she had a stroke. I had to work late and went home first to fix dinner, but I had called her and told her earlier in the day that I wouldn't be able to come over and see her until later in the evening. After dinner, I came back to Pleasant Grove to visit her. When I got there, I couldn't find her, and she wasn't in her room. Her roommate said she never came back from dinner, so I went down to the dining room, and it was all closed up. I couldn't find her. I asked one of the workers there, and they said to try in the TV room next door. I went there, but there was nobody else there. My mom was sitting in

Me and my Mom

her wheelchair, and her head was kind of down, and I said, "Mom?" She didn't respond. She didn't even know who she was, she didn't even know who I was, she didn't talk, she didn't do anything. I called the nurses, and they came. We got her back into her bedroom. Turns out, she had had a stroke, and she wasn't coherent. Then, she went into a coma.

They changed her medication that day, and I guess her body reacted adversely to it, and she had a stroke because of that. We didn't know if she was going to come out of it. She lasted a few days, and then, she got pneumonia on top of this. She had told me time and time again that she did not want to be given medicine to keep her alive. She lived a really good life and everything, and when it was her time to go, she just wanted to go, so I told him that. It was in her papers at the nursing home to keep her comfortable and not give anything to prolong life, but make sure she's not in pain and that she's very comfortable. So, she was like this for several days, and they said it would be a few days before she probably passes away. We kind of waited, and they called from the nursing home one evening and said, "I think that she's made some different changes in her behavior, and we don't think it's going to be very long for her to pass away. So, you might need to get the family together, and come over and say your good-byes."

We got all the kids together and went over to the nursing home. She didn't even recognize us. Everybody took turns going up to her to tell her they loved her. It was a sad time. Everybody was crying because we knew we might not see her again. I was the last one to go up. Everybody in the family knows I'm an emotional mess, but I just went up and put my arm around her. I told her: I want you to know I could not have had a better mom, and I love you so much and so I want you to know that we'll be fine here, and we want you to be able to see Dad. I told her how much I cared for her and what a great mother she was. At that point, a tear fell down from her eye and ran down her cheek. Now, everybody saw it. It didn't seem possible because of the stroke and the coma, but it happened. They said she was probably going to die within the next 24 hours, but she lasted two more weeks. So, we visited her again, but the second time wasn't as sad because we thought really, we don't know when she's going to die. One morning, I got a call at school, and they said she had just passed away. My aunt was over there at the nursing home, sitting with her, and she just took a deep breath and stopped breathing, so it was very peaceful.

CHAPTER 3: EARLY YEARS

My First House on Henderson Ave (Audio Vol. 4)

This picture is of the house I lived in after I was adopted. My grandpa owned the house and had lived there with his son Cecil and his wife Lilian Cordelia Garren Day before she passed away. My Aunt Gertrude, Cecil's sister, also grew up in this house, but by the time I entered the picture, she had already graduated from college and was a teacher. I lived my early life at 595 Henderson Avenue. That house was, as I remember it, a medium gray stucco. It had a great big porch on it, and my grandpa used to love to sit on the porch to smoke as my mom didn't like smoke in the house. We had a great big pine tree in the front yard. We didn't have sidewalks, but we had grass that went all the way to the road.

The neighbor across the street had the same type of front yard, but he had corrals and barns with cows and horses at the back of his house. He raised dairy cows, and we got our milk

Me & my Mexican Sombrero in front of Henderson House

from him. When I was five years old, my job was to go across the street and get milk from his house every day. I remember taking this path along the side of their house to the backyard, and there were Bougainvillea bushes. In the afternoon when I would have to go get the milk, the dragon flies would dart in and out of the bushes and fly close to your face and hair. I hated it and would start running when I got to that part of the path and wouldn't stop until I got to the front of his property. That's what I remember about getting milk! His name was Roy Hardy; he had an older daughter that lived with him, and he became a really good friend to our family (especially my grandpa). He would often come over and talk to my grandpa on the front porch.

As I mentioned before, we had a very large pine tree in our front yard, and it was rumored that there were a lot of snakes living in it. We lived in a rural area, and there were snakes in the fields around our house. The neighbor kids would dare each other to climb to the top of the pine tree. I avoided the tree like a plague because I was scared of snakes. I didn't want to even go near the tree, but it was right by the sidewalk that went from our front door out to the street. One day, I was coming home from school, and there was this great big king snake that was slithering up the sidewalk. My grandpa was sitting on the front porch, and he was watching me while he chatted with his friend. The friend had to go home eventually, so his focus shifted to me. I got halfway up the sidewalk and could see the snake already. I didn't know what to do; it made me nervous to go around the snake, so my grandpa went and got a shovel. He walked up to the snake and chopped off his head with one swing. It made me so nervous, seeing that slithering thing flailing itself around before it finally went still. My grandpa very carefully picked up the snake with the shovel and put it in the garbage can, shutting the lid tightly. You see, it was very normal for Grandpa to do things like that. But I do remember it clearly because it had such an impact on me when I was young.

Henderson Avenue was in a rural area of town and there were not a lot of neighbors. In fact, our house was on a corner lot and most of the people we knew were across the street from the front of our house or across the street from the side of our house. There were two families that had kids around my age that I played with quite a bit, but I was also very comfortable playing alone. I had lots of dolls, most of which were made by my mom. As I would play outside I remember sitting on the bumper of our old Plymouth car and setting a little table out there, so I could feed and have tea parties with my dolls.

Sue & her dolls

I remember another thing about our house on Henderson Avenue – our kitchen sink was really high. When I was little, I remember I couldn't wait to become tall enough to do the dishes without having to stand on a chair. My dad would always do the dishes because my mom would do the cooking. It was a rule that when my mom cooked, my dad would do the dishes, and it was my job to rinse and dry the dishes. Because I wasn't tall enough to reach the sink, I would have to stand on a chair.

We also had a wood stove in our house, which is what I remember the most. We didn't have an electric or gas stove. We had a large wood-burning stove that you could cook on top of with a large oven. My mom would bake bread in it each week. In the winter it was great because the stove would keep the kitchen warm and cozy. We had an old Plymouth car that my mom named Betsy, and we would park it at the back of the house where the barn and corrals were. My dad had cows and chickens and a large garden, which he was very proud of. We had neighbors across the street and others that were down the street to the side of our house. There were two families that had kids close to my age. One boy I remember walked home from school with me each day since he lived down the street from me; his name was Derlan German. Coming home from school, we walked over a large bridge that spanned over several train tracks. We loved to stand and watch the trains go under the bridge. I remember one of Derlan's favorite things to do was pee on top of the trains as they went under the bridge (which I thought was disgusting).

Mrs. Horn, a dear neighbor on Henderson Ave. & me at 2-3 months

Mrs. Horn also lived down the street from us. She was an older lady who was like a grandma to me. She was so excited for my mom and dad when they brought me home. When I was four or five years old, I loved to visit her in her trailer. I remember she used to make interesting pictures out of butterflies or small bugs and flowers that she would dry in the middle of books. She would then arrange them in an abalone shell or a picture frame, or she would make them into necklaces or broaches to sell to people. I thought they were so beautiful, and she would let me watch her work. I used to love to go to her house, and she would tell me stories about when she was a little girl. She would let me come in and talk for hours. Those probably are the people that I remember most about the neighborhood in the house on Henderson Avenue.

The house on Henderson Avenue had three bedrooms. I had a bedroom to myself. My mom and dad shared one, and my grandpa had the other one. It wasn't a very large house, but I remember the dining room which was right off the living room. We had a big round table made of oak. It belonged to Grandpa and Grandma Day. It had two ends that could be added to make it bigger when we had company for dinner. The kitchen was next to the dining room at the back of the house with a door to the backyard, and I remember it being quite big. We had light pink bougainvillea bushes that grew close to the side of the house outside the kitchen. The robins liked to build their nests in those bushes. We had to watch when the robins would build their nests and lay their eggs because when the eggs would hatch they were a prime target for the snakes from the surrounding fields and the snakes could be seen slithering up the bougainvillea bushes to eat the baby birds. The front of the house had an enclosed porch where my grandpa would like to sit and watch what was going on in the neighborhood.

I attended Fremont Elementary School for kindergarten, first grade, and second grade until Christmas vacation. The thing that I remember most about kindergarten was rest time. We used to have naps on a mat that we would get out of our locker, roll out on the floor, and lay down on to rest. I used to sometimes pretend to be asleep, so the teacher wouldn't get me up, and I would just keep pretending while she finished teaching. I don't know why I remember that, but I just remember I thought it was so smart that she didn't know I wasn't really asleep. In kindergarten, I can't remember much except that I loved to paint. In second grade, I remember moving to a new school during Christmas vacation. My new school was Teach Elementary. It was a lot different from Fremont Elementary which was much older. Teach Elementary was a new school that had only been open for a few years. All the doors to the classrooms opened up to the outside.

At that time, our family moved to 876 Venable Street. We moved from the house on Henderson Avenue because the city came and said they were going to build a freeway through the part of town where our house was. They offered to pay my grandpa to buy the house, so we found our new home and moved during my Christmas break.

Pictures of Me When I Lived on Henderson Ave

My Blessing Day

Sue & her Stuffed Animal Friends

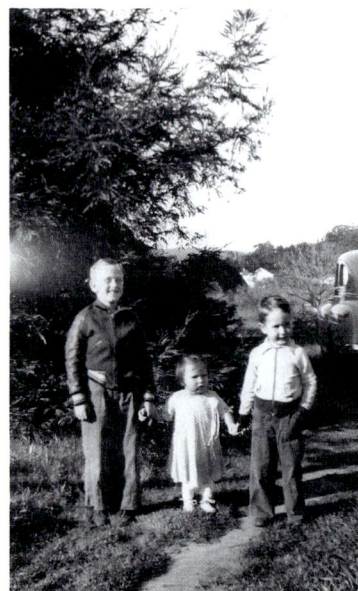

Sue with Cousins David & Al Hoslett by Pine Tree

Sue by large Pine Tree at Henderson House

Sue & her dolls

Sue as a Flower Girl for Cousin LaRae & Kenneth's Wedding

My Second House on Venable St. (Audio Vol 3)

This is a picture of the house where I lived from second grade all the way up until I went away for college. It still exists on 876 Venable Street in San Luis Obispo, California. I recognize some things about the house, but it has changed a lot from when we sold it after my dad passed away. I noticed it still has a lemon tree in the front yard, but the current owners have changed the driveway to brick pavers. Also, the porch was altered a little with a railing going down the side of the front steps. The house is now gray stucco instead of white. The front door has been painted green. The porch is where I used to prop up my bike while learning how to ride. I was given a used boys bike that was a little tall for me, and I couldn't quite reach the pedals. I would lean the bike up against the porch, get the pedal up at the top, then push it really hard so it would go fast, and that's how I kept my balance until I learned how to balance better.

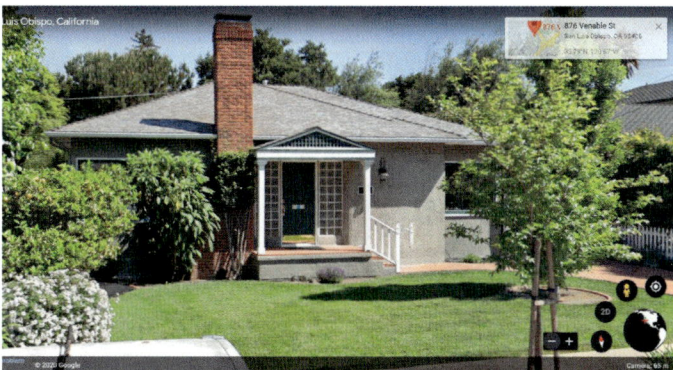
My house on 876 Venable Street

My grandpa bought this house, so we could all still live together. His bedroom was in the front of the house on the right side. He stayed in there a lot because he was a chain smoker, and my mom said he could only smoke in his bedroom or in a chair on the front porch. A side note about my grandpa's room was after he died, my mom decided to paint his room. His room was originally a light blue and because of the

19

Another view of the Venable house

Learning to ride my new bike on Venable St

smoking in his room, the walls were a yellow green. The house had a long driveway which wound around the house to the back. We had an orchard on one side of our house and on the other side was our neighbor – a single mom with two daughters. Across the street from our house was a young family with a little girl. Ed and Betty Simmons became very good friends with my mom and dad, and I loved to go over and visit with Betty and their little girl, who they called Chickie. Betty grew up in Paso Robles. Her dad owned a bakery, and she would help him. She learned how to make a lot of pastries and was very good at decorating cakes. In fact, Betty and her dad made my wedding cake.

Ed and Betty had another daughter named Kristy. When I got older, I got to babysit the two girls. I have a lot of good memories about their family. They were really good to my parents the whole time we lived there. Next door to the Simmons' house was the Kendalls'. Their dad was a Methodist minister in the community. They had several children; the oldest two girls were Heidi and Leilani. They were such a good, caring family. If anyone got sick in our household, Elsa, the mom, would bring us dinner. Their family always watched over ours. I even went to Bible School in the summer with their kids, and Heidi and Leilani went to Primary with me.

Me playing the piano at the Venable house

Our Venable Street house had a fireplace in the front of the house. It was where my mom would build a fire every morning and then sit and play solitaire. In San Luis Obispo, there was fog until about 11 o'clock. I had to get up to go to Seminary early in the morning, and I would stand there and get warmed up by the fire before I'd have breakfast.

I have a lot of good memories of living on Venable Street. We had an all-ages carpool that took four people from our street to school. It was a really friendly neighborhood. Now, the end of the street has been turned into a cul-de-sac, but when I lived there, it was a vacant lot. They used to have these different religious groups come there with big tents, and they'd have these revivals. So, the neighbor kids and I would sneak under the bottom of the tent and watch them as they would shout and sing and even roll on the

Teach School Elementary where I attended from 2nd-6th grade

floor at times; it was definitely an experience to watch. We had another vacant lot on the street, and it had big potholes in it. When it rained, the holes would fill with water. So, we used to put on these big boots, and we would go and jump into the big potholes of water. Venable Street had a lot of great memories for me with night games, biking, building stilts and learning to walk on them, and a lot of kids to play with. There were the Symons, the Pools, the Marcums, the Kendalls, and some others that moved in later. I lived there until I left for college at BYU when I was 18 years old.

Moving to 876 Venable Street during Christmas break was both exciting and scary at the same time. I transferred to Teach Elementary School which was a lot different from Fremont because it was a lot more modern. All of our classroom doors faced outside. I remember in my second grade I learned square dancing. My teacher was Mrs. Delatore. It was the first time we had to dance with boys. It was such a weird thing – how you had to hold the boy's hand when you were dancing, and the boys would make such a big fuss about it, but it turned out to be really fun.

My third-grade teacher, I had her twice. I had her again in the sixth grade. Her name was Mrs. Butzbach. During elementary school, I was a member of Bluebirds and Camp Fire Girls. It wasn't a church-related thing, but we did a lot of service projects, and it was a good thing. I remember we had a uniform, so we got to wear this little jumper kind of thing on the days we had class. I learned a lot of things, including a little bit with animals. Overall, it was a really good experience.

My Baptism

When I was approaching 8 years old, I had been learning about being baptized

Me with our branch in front of the Church house

into the Church of Jesus Christ of Latter-day Saints of which my parents were members. In Primary and Sunday School we had a lot of lessons concerning baptism. I knew that I wanted to be baptized but I was scared. I knew that I loved Jesus and that He had been baptized and He said it was important to be baptized.

The baptismal font was in the basement of our church building. It was in a small room, up a few stairs with a large heater in it. The font was constructed of wood in a large tub-like shape. There was only room enough for about 4-5 people to stand in the room to witness the baptism. My dad wanted to baptize me which he had never done before. I was really nervous.

Sister Godfrey came over to talk to me to try and reassure me that it was not scary. At that point I did not know how to swim and I was afraid to go under water so I was in a dilemma. I had known Sister Godfrey ever since I could remember and I trusted her. She said she had something for me if I would be brave and go through with it. I did go through it and I was so happy. She slipped a dime in my hand and said she was proud of me. President Godfrey confirmed me a member of The Church of Jesus Christ of Latter-day Saints and blessed me to receive the Holy Ghost. That is the best gift I have ever received.

Finding Out About My Adoption

I was at home one day, and we got a phone call. It was a man on the phone, and he said, "Is this the Day residence where the Chinese girl lives?" And I said "No, you must have the wrong number." And so, he hung up. Several minutes went by, and he called back and asked to speak to my mother. I was really kind of curious about the whole thing. When he got off the phone with my mother, I asked my mom, "Why was he talking about a Chinese girl?" She said, "Well, we need to have a talk." So, we sat down, and she told me I was part Chinese and that I was adopted when I was a little baby.

The whole thing just shocked me. I didn't know I was adopted. It brought up a lot of questions in my mind about why I was adopted. Why did my mother not want me? But then I thought, Chinese… I'm Chinese and I never ever thought I was Chinese. My mom told me how much they loved me and how they were unable to have children, and so they wanted to adopt me. I lived with them for a long time, and eventually, they felt that I was the right person for their family.

Anyway, that was a big change in my life, and it took me a little while to kind of digest all of this, but it turned out to be really good. I learned how important it was and how special it was. I learned how lucky I was to have someone to care for me and love me because if this had not happened, I could have gone somewhere else or been a foster child because I was a ward of the court. It all turned out well, and I grew up in that home and knew I had a place to stay forever.

AH Louis store that my parents took me to

Around that age, we started going to dinner once a month in Chinatown. Chinatown in San Luis Obispo was just one street. There were a couple of restaurants and other Chinese stores that sold different merchandise. My mom and dad would take me once a month after my dad got his paycheck, and we would go eat at a Chinese restaurant. I loved it. My favorite thing was when I would ask for fried turtles. We would joke about it because when I was really little, I thought the fried shrimp looked like turtles. And the waitress knew us by heart because we came every month. That was a special time for us to go out, and then, we would always go across the street to this store. It was called the "AH LOUIS" store and it was owned by this couple who had come over from mainland China and had all sorts of things embodying China. One section had different and unique toys. There were some made with string and little clam shells, and you would put them into water and watch them open

Mrs. Butzbach's class

up, and little things would come out of the clam shells. I loved them. There were just all different kinds of things. So, the head of the store would always take me over there and let me choose something every time I'd go. It was always such a special time with just me and my mom and dad.

Memorizing poems written by famous people was one of Mrs. Butzbach's favorite things in her class. I remember the notebook I had with all sorts of poetry by such authors as Robert Frost and Edgar A. Guest and many others. Reciting them in front of the class was the part I didn't like so much, but I do still remember parts of the poems.

Another thing I remember about Elementary School and Mrs. Butzbach was playing Jacks. We would have Jacks tournaments, and we would sit down on the playground and compete with different groups. It was so fun.

After sixth grade, we went to junior high. They had a new junior high that was only a few years old. It was across town and up on a hill. In fact, the senior high was down the hill, and there were a bunch of steps from the senior high up to the junior high. Then, in the middle, there was a big cafeteria. Because we were on different schedules, the junior high schoolers would eat there part of the time, and the senior high schoolers had a different lunch time. Junior high was really fun, but in the middle of junior high, they had to close the senior high school to make it earthquake-proof. I guess they were doing this all over San Luis Obispo. Anyway, the junior high would go in the morning, and the senior high would go in the afternoon.

My Grandpa Day

When I was a senior, I got a job as a secretary for the Institute of Religion in San Luis Obispo. I would go there and work in the morning as a secretary for Frank Bradshaw, and then, I would go to school in the afternoon.   Working for Br. Bradshaw was a really good experience. We had a lot of good talks, and I got to be a secretary and write to all these important people in the church. Br. Bradshaw was the Institute Director for Cal Poly and the college students would come by to talk to him which was a highlight for me.

About this time too, in high school, is when my mom and dad said they would like to have me sealed to them. They waited so long because they wanted me to be able to choose. That was a big thing, I mean, to choose if I really wanted to be sealed to them for all eternity. Usually, it's not a decision for children because you're just born into the covenant and you're with them forever, but if you're adopted, you have to be sealed to them. And so, I had to think about it a lot and pray about it, and I concluded that they were my parents. Why wouldn't I want to be sealed to them? So, we decided to do this.

My grandpa lived with us until I was about 13 years old. He was a chain smoker, a retired man, and a bit self-absorbed. My mom took care of him, cleaned his room, cut his hair, cooked all his food, and pressed his clothes. She did everything for him. His health was never good. He did not like the church and had some issues with the missionaries. They would come over every week for dinner at our house, and he would give them a

Sealing to my parents in the Los Angeles Temple

hard time about the church. He and I would always get in a fight about how rude he was to the missionaries.

He died when I was 13. That morning, I was learning how to sew. My mom had an old sewing machine, and I was learning how to put in a zipper in a dress I was making. While I was working on it, my mom said, "Well, it's time for breakfast, go and get Grandpa." I usually would always go get him for breakfast. But, I was in the middle of my task and asked if she could get him instead. And so, she went in to get Grandpa and found him slumped over the side of the bed. He had passed away in the night. The miracle of the whole thing was that he was smoking a cigarette at the time he died, and the cigarette burned a hole all the way through his desk by the side of his bed. It went through the desk and made it to the floor, and it burned a little hole in the floor and went out. I remember thinking, "Oh my heavens! It could have burned the whole house down!" Anyway, my mom very calmly came out of the bedroom and told me what had happened. She said she had to call the doctor and the mortuary to come and get him. The whole thing really freaked me out, so I ran over to the neighbor who was a Methodist Minister. I went to their house because I didn't even want to see him brought out and put in the ambulance. I did go to the funeral, but I didn't even want to look at him in the casket because it just terrorized me. For years, I had this issue with dead bodies. It took me until after I was married, and I was in the Relief Society Presidency while we were living in Eau Claire, Wisconsin to get over it. When you live in the mission field and there's a death of some-

body that has been through the temple, and the family wants them buried in their Temple clothes, the Relief Society Presidency has to do it. I was petrified. We all fasted and prayed before we went, and I prayed that I could just get through it without passing out on the floor. I was a nervous wreck. But it turned out to be a wonderful experience. We had three people die that year and had to dress their bodies, and it became a real spiritual experience. It was like the last thing you could do for that person on this side of the veil, and even though they weren't there in spirit, it was a service we performed for them.

All right, now back to the story about me choosing to go to the temple when I was around 15. My parents didn't just spring it on me; they had told me they wanted to be sealed to me several years before and gave me time to think about it. So, we decided to do it. The closest temple was the Los Angeles Temple, and it was about 200 miles south of San Luis Obispo. So, all the people that wanted to go do temple work for the day chartered a bus. We packed a lunch, and took the bus down to the Los Angeles Temple. My mom and dad not only did sealings for me to be sealed to them, but they also did the sealings for my grandpa and grandma to be sealed to my dad and to each other. I had to go to the nursery and because I was the oldest one, I had to help with all the babies. People usually have their baby or child sealed to them when they're little, not when they are 15. It turned out to be a very sacred experience. I was not totally prepared for the temple clothing because I never had had that experience before, but my mom explained it to me when we were there. It's a sacred place where you feel the spirit and you know you're doing the right thing. So, that's when I became sealed to them. I was grateful for the time that I had, and it meant so much to them as well.

Memorable Foods Growing Up (Audio Vol. 54)

As far as food in my family went, we had a very limited budget. We used a lot of cheaper cuts of meat and vegetables. My dad had a garden. I remember my dad loved liver and onions, which I'm not too fond of, but I know we had it a certain night every week. I learned that if you have a lot of onions on it and you put a lot of Ketchup on it, then it's pretty good. Another thing my dad would make was homemade oyster stew. He would make it every Sunday night, and I never got a taste for that. I hated oysters, and so, I would always make chicken noodle soup or something out of a can when he would make oyster stew. Another thing is that we'd always have sauerkraut and weenies. I grew to love sauerkraut.

My mom would make homemade bread, and she would give it to any family, friends, or neighbors who were sick. She would leave one in the mailbox for the mailman, and she would give one to the milkman when he would deliver the milk the next morning.

We would make about 10 loaves a week, so when a batch was ready to come out of the oven, we'd be ready with butter and honey and would cut a big slice, and cover the bread while it was still hot. It was the best! My mom made the best bread ever, and we would eat a whole loaf right as it got out of the oven, before we would even eat dinner because it was just so good. My mom was well known for her great bread. When she got really bad arthritis as she got older, she couldn't knead the bread. It was before they had automatic machines that kneaded the bread, so I took over that job. I would have to knead 10 pounds of flour to make bread every week, but the bread was awesome. We would have a lot of beef stew, and other soups and beans but we would always have her good bread to go with it. It always tasted good, and if it didn't, I would always add Ketchup.

So, those are some of the things that we would have. My mom would make cookies too. She cooked all the time because she grew up on a farm, and she knew how to make everything from scratch, so I grew up with that and loved all of the things that she made. She was a great cook.

But as far as purchasing things at the store other than the ingredients for the bread, she became really good friends with the butcher and with the produce man at the grocery store. We had a little grocery store near our house that I would either ride my bike to or we would drive there. We knew the day of the week they would put produce out that was getting a little bit old. It would usually go into a box in the garbage. It was a great big garbage bin at the back of the store, and so my mom would consult with the produce man, and we would pick out the good things and take them home.

She would also have the butcher save her cuts of meat that were maybe a little older. They weren't bad yet, but they would be marked so you could get them a lot cheaper. He would save them, and my mom would pick from those. I grew up that way, and nobody ever knew anything, even when we would have people over for dinner all the time. I just thought it was a way of life. So, for me, to go dumpster diving and get things out of the garbage was kind of a fun thing. Another thing we used to do is when we took a trip to the dump, there'd be furniture out there, old pots, and all kinds of things. We would go out there and look around, and we'd always find some wonderful things that we could repurpose at our house. So, you asked – did we have enough money growing up? Yes, we did, but we probably got around a lot of things in a different way than most people do. And we did not go on welfare from the church, which my mom and dad were very proud of. And so, we made do with what we could.

CHAPTER 4: TEENAGE YEARS AND COLLEGE

My High School Years

Jane Murray and I after church

In high school, I became a Seminary President. Our seminary wasn't functioning until my junior year in high school. They only had seminary in San Luis Obispo for my junior and senior years, and during my senior year, I became the Stake Seminary President for our whole stake which was a good experience.

It's not like it was a huge area, but we had to travel to all the different places, and I got some good experiences. I spoke in stake conferences, which petrified me, but I got to speak in some different seminaries and visit many different places, so it turned out to be a really good experience. It helped me increase my testimony a lot. Therefore, I became closer to the Lord.

My mom was worried that I was going to marry some non-Mormon because there were very few LDS guys in San Luis Obispo so when I met this guy Dave at a stake dance, she was thrilled. His father was even in the stake presidency. They lived in Santa Maria, so he would drive up to see me all the time. We would go to a movie or some church or school activity. I dated him for the rest of high school, and my mom was thrilled because she thought for sure I was going to marry him. It was an answer to her prayers about me finding somebody that was a member of the church. We became really good friends. I went to his dances, and he came up and went to mine. We went to each other's

Me by Mom's poinsettia

Me by Venable house

My Senior picture

graduations.

When it came time for me to go to college, I wanted to stay around there. Dave was going to college down in Santa Maria, But, my mom was very insistent I go to BYU because she said I needed some other experiences that I wasn't having in San Luis Obispo. We kind of agreed that we would still date other people and not just be exclusive with each other since he and I were in different towns.

When I got to college, Dave surprised me one time coming up to visit me during my freshman year. It was in the fall, and I had a date with a guy from the University of Utah. We went to his homecoming, so I got a late pass, and Dave had come up to surprise me. He had taken off work that Friday and drove all the way from Santa Maria to Provo to surprise me, but I wasn't home. So, he took my roommates to the movies and to dinner. I had taken a late pass out that night, so I didn't get home until 2:00 am. When I got in the dorm, my roommate told me Dave was waiting in the parking lot . So, I went to my dorm mom and said, "I know I had a late pass, but this guy came up from California to see me, and I haven't even been able to see him." She let me stay out for one more hour. I went and saw him, and we talked, but that was kind of the beginning of the end of our relationship. He was really quite upset, and he had started dating this girl down in Santa Maria. Eventually, he went on a mission, and she waited for him. He married her, and I went a different path. We remained good friends, and he even visited me after I was married to Brent.

In front of my dorm at Knight Mangum Hall

Jobs Growing Up (Audio Vol. 15, 46 & 47)

I had some interesting jobs in high school. The first one I had was working in the San Luis Obispo County Hospital as a "tray girl." The title sounds kind of weird, but it was the physically hardest job I have ever had because literally I went to work at seven in the morning, I was on my feet all day, even through breaks and lunch, until I got off at six. I couldn't even leave until I got all the dishes done for the next morning. My stake president is the one that got me the job. He was also the assistant principal of the high school where I went, and he called me one day and said he found me a job. If I were looking for a job, he found a good one for me, but the bad thing was that I had to work on Sundays. I always thought it was kind of interesting that my stake president got me a job where I worked on Sundays, but in a way, it kind of strengthened my testimony. I really missed going to church. I don't know if I had really ever missed going to church before that, but it really kind of solidified the rest of my life about how important I felt it was to go to church. As a tray girl, I had to make salads and help with the preparation, but I also had to check all the little notes on the trays for the different patients. So, if they needed low salt or had high blood pressure, I had to make sure they had the right foods and weren't getting anything wrong on their trays. This was a small part of what I did because I worked non-stop all day, and then, we had to do the dishes after every meal. It was just go, go, go.

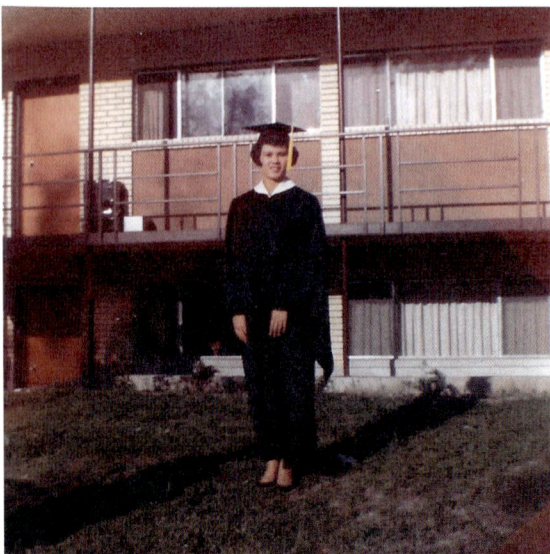

My college graduation picture

The next job I had was a motel maid. It wasn't a high-end motel, but it wasn't a low-end motel either. I remember I had to go around to so many rooms per day and clean all the rooms and make the beds. Some people were really messy, and I had to clean up all their trash, from beer bottles and cigarettes to all kinds of stuff. By the end of the day, my back would hurt from making beds and picking up dirty laundry and garbage. It was a definite change in what I was used to doing.

I was also a secretary to an insurance agent at one point. The owner would go to India and South America to shoot big game like tigers and lions for his hobby. He had skins on the walls of his office that he had shot, and so, the letters that I got to type and send were interesting because they were to people that I wouldn't normally ever correspond with.

Another job I had was the institute secretary when our high school was shut down and we had to go to the junior high building. We went for half the day during my senior year in the morning. I didn't go to school, so I worked at the LDS Institute that serviced Cal Poly students which was in part of our church building. I worked as a secretary in the mornings, and then in the afternoons, from 12 to 5, I would go to school. I would also clean some older ladies' houses in the ward and babysit for friends and neighbors. All of these experiences helped to build my character and I realized what kinds of jobs I didn't want to do in life.

Junior High Experiences

I remember that moving to junior high from elementary school was a big adjustment. I had a lot of friends in elementary school, but in junior high, some of them remained friends, and some changed. I became friends with some people that went into student government. They were really interested in it, so we would either be on the school council or secretary. I was a secretary for a while in junior high. We were really good friends during eighth grade and ninth grade. These friends were really good people, but they started having a lot of parties, and then eventually, they started bringing beer to the parties. I felt really uncomfortable with this, and I didn't really say anything. I'd always make excuses for not drinking and I'd always bring a can of pop or something. I went to several of the parties, but it was getting harder to really have fun because of our different values. Eventually, I just stopped going to the parties. I'd make up some reasons why I couldn't, and my mom said she could help me make up things too because she could feel that I was really uncomfortable. I had real open communication with my mom, and I would tell her what they did and how uncomfortable I felt. She let me make my own decisions on these things, and she would give me a lot of counsel, but then, she'd let me decide. I always knew what was right. But, sometimes you make the wrong decision before you make the right decision, and that's what happened in this case. I started dropping out of their parties and not going to them, and I started hanging out with a totally different group of friends, which were not the popular group. My new friends were just average kids. One lived a couple streets down from us and we like to hang out. Her name was Sandra, and she wasn't a member of our church, but she went to a church, and she had good basic values. We started to do things on our own, and eventually, I just kind of dropped away from those other friends, even though I would still talk to them in the hall. I would just say I had other things to do.

This experience had a long-lasting effect on me because I was able to do this and kind of get away from these people and still be friends but not really close friends. I started to determine my value system and along the way, I realized that I didn't feel comfortable with what they were doing. I knew it was the wrong thing to do, and I just didn't feel comfortable with those friends. And so, sometimes in life, we have to evaluate where or who we are hanging around with and decide if it's really good for us or if it's better that we maybe make a change and seek out other people. You sometimes think, "Oh, my heavens, my life is so lonely because I don't have any friends." But it doesn't take too much time and things open up. You can develop new friends, and they can become a very good influence on the rest of your life

CHAPTER 5: OUR COURTSHIP AND ENGAGEMENT

How I Met Brent (Audio Vol. 54)

I would like to tell you my version of how Brent and I met in college. It started in my junior year, and he dated my roommate Carolyn. She had just broken up with the boyfriend she had, and I don't know how she met Brent, but they started going out together. Carolyn was always late for dates, and she was never ready when he would come to pick her up. I lived in Heritage Halls at the time with five other roommates. So, Brent had to sit out there in the foyer to wait for her. I would go down and talk to him, and then, we would go down to the basement and play ping-pong while Carolyn got ready. That's how I met him, and we became good friends and talked a lot. Well, that summer, Carolyn broke up with him. I don't know what happened. She was at home, and I guess it was a mutually agreeable situation. Anyway, they weren't dating anymore, and it was summer. I was at home working in the summertime. In the fall, I went back to college for my senior year. I rode up with a bunch of kids from San Luis Obispo. Some of the people in the car did not have housing yet, so we went to the administration building. We all looked grubby because we'd driven straight through for 16 hours. I went into the administration building with them to show where the board was that listed all of the apartments and housing available. As I was going in, Brent was coming out of the administration building. I don't know what he was doing up there, but he had given his friend Frank Apalonio a ride up there. We started talking and I mentioned that I heard about his and Carolyn's break up. Then, he started asking what I was up to with school this year. And I said, "Well I'm actually going to be in Salt Lake this year because I'm doing my student teaching up there, and so a bunch of us that are teaching up there got an apartment together and we're living up there for the semester." He said, " My folks live up there." I said, "Oh really? Well, if you're ever up that way, to see your folks... Let me give you my phone number and you can give me a call. We can go get something to eat or do something else.." It was just a very casual conversation because we were good friends and felt comfortable together. I didn't hear from him until October, before General Conference. Brent was in charge of the Irish Missionary Reunion that year. He invited me to join him. So, we went there on our first date. It was not too memorable because he was in charge. He was running around doing all these things to make sure everything went well, and I sat and talked to a bunch of girls that were there with other missionaries.

That was kind of the beginning, and from then on, every time he came to Salt

Lake, he called me and asked me out. We dated through the fall. Sometimes, I would go down to BYU, and sometimes, he would come up there. One time we were down in Provo and we went to Bridal Veil Falls. He was really quite more serious at that point than I was. I mean, I did really, really like him, but I wasn't ready to commit to marriage. I had a missionary that was in Holland, and he wrote to me every week, and we were good friends as well. However, things got more serious as we dated every weekend. I eventually wrote to my missionary to explain how things were. And as a result, we broke up. As it got closer to Christmas, I decided to invite Brent to San Luis Obispo to meet my mom and dad and see where I grew up.

Later on, Brent asked me to marry him on New Year's Eve. It was really freezing out. I remember it was supposed to be a really romantic evening, and Brent said, "Oh I want to take you to this beautiful place. I have something to ask you." We got there, and I just had a light sweater on. It was so cold; the wind was blowing hard, and it was starting to snow. We got out of the car; Brent took me over to a place between the Seagull Monument and Handcart Monument on Temple Square in downtown Salt Lake City. He started to tell me how he felt about me and how he had fallen in love with me. I said, "I'm sorry, I don't mean to be rude, but could we finish this conversation in the car?" I really wanted him to finish, but I was shivering. It was just so cold. We ended up getting back in the car and turning up the heater, and it was there he gave me my engagement ring. I was very happy and excited to show my roommates my ring. So anyway, that was the beginning of our relationship. From then on, it just progressed, and we worked out the kinks and everything, and we ended up getting married in June.

CHAPTER 6: OUR WEDDING

Planning our wedding got a little crazy. I was to graduate in the last part of May from BYU. My mom and dad wanted to be in Utah for both events, and since my dad's health wasn't too good at the time, we decided to have the two events close together. It was so important to my dad that he got to see me graduate from college since he or my mother had only completed the 8th grade. We all made it through my graduation and then looked forward to our next event, our wedding.

We planned to be married in the Manti Temple on June 5 as it was the temple where Brent's Grandma Peterson lived and it was close to Centerfield where Brent grew up. We planned to have our wedding luncheon in Gunnison at the Wisteria Cafe following our temple ceremony. That evening was to be our

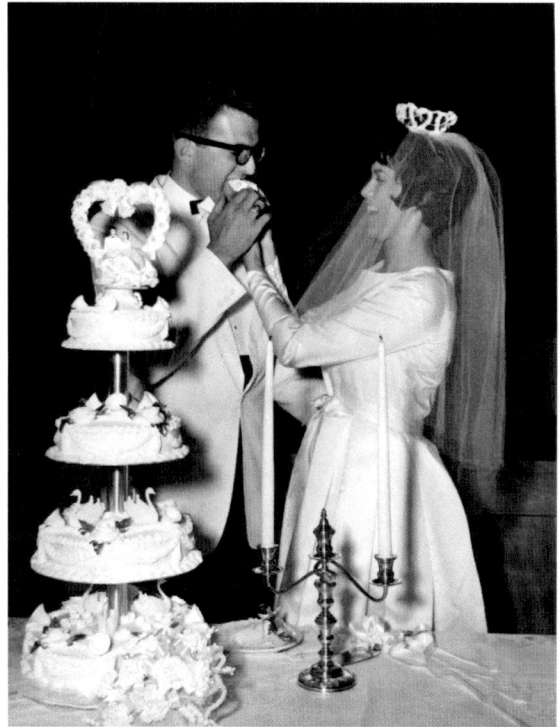

Wedding reception in San Luis Obispo

Wedding Reception. It was to be held at the Centerfield Ward Building that evening.

Everything went according to plan. The temple ceremony was beautiful; we were sealed by a cousin of Brent's mom. I had taken my endowments out earlier on my mom's birthday, May 18, in the Salt Lake Temple. Since Brent was already endowed, we had just the sealing ceremony on June 5. I was nervous about the ceremony, but the temple matrons did everything to make me feel calm and be able to focus on the event. It was a beautiful day, and both of her parents were there as well as Brent's sisters and other extended family. I remember the feeling of peace and happiness I felt in the temple that day.

The luncheon went according to plan with just close family and a few friends in attendance. Wisteria Cafe was a good selection since Brent's family was very familiar with the place and knew the people who ran it. The rest of the afternoon was spent adding

Dancing at my wedding

the finishing touches to the hall where the reception was to be held.

Before the reception, pictures were taken of the bridal party. A funny incident happened with Brent. He picked up his Dad's coat for the pictures which was a different color than Brent's suit. So when we look at the pictures of our Centerfield reception, we just have a chuckle.

At the reception, we had a line, but then we had a program and a tribute to the bride and groom and a response from the bride and groom. This was all new to me, but it was nice. We also had a musical number from Gerald Torgason, who was a friend of Brent's. He was an amazing man who was blind, but so gifted in so many ways. It was a beautiful program which was made possible by the kind people of Centerfield who put some much time and effort into the evening. Another aspect of a Centerfield wedding/reception that was unfamiliar to me is the way gifts are purchased. In Gunnison, at Christensen's Department Store, there is a sign-up list that has several items on it. People can pay what they want to and can contribute any amount to a designated list, signing the card so the bride & groom knew who contributed to the gift. So, in other words, 20 people could be listed as giving a group of items. I loved it!

We took our honeymoon traveling from Centerfield to San Luis Obispo, stopping at the Grand Canyon and Las Vegas. The Grand Canyon was beautiful. The only downside was losing our camera on a bench when we stopped to rest a bit. Las Vegas was exciting. We got to see some good shows as well as eat delicious food. Only one show was a bit risque!!!!!

The reception in San Luis Obispo was a work of love, mostly by my mom and good friends and neighbors. Our neighbor, Betty Symons and her Dad, made my wedding cake; Norm Seid, a college student who lived with us for awhile made the forms for my cake; the Schroeders, our next door neighbor, took all of our pictures; my mom made my wedding dress; and my cousin, David Hoslett's wife made my veil. Various friends and neighbors decorated the cultural hall and arranged for the music and girls from our ward to do all the serving. Everyone donated their time and resources because they loved my mom.

My maid of honor was Lynne Greenall, my best friend, and my bridesmaids were

Naomi Jacobs, my roommate; Wardeen Phelps, a friend from San Luis Obispo; Karen, Brent's sister.

One funny incident that happened at our San Luis Obispo reception was concerning a guest. Brent's mom's cousin had a few too many drinks before coming to our reception. He went through our wedding line several times before we caught him. He was kissing each bridesmaid on the lips. After complaints from the bridesmaids, we escorted him out of the room.

Me ad my wedding with both sets of parents

And the rest of the reception went through without any problems. We had a small band that was local and known by some friends, with dancing. We had the reception in the cultural hall of our church building and a good time was had by all.

CHAPTER 7: TEACHING SCHOOL
AND MARRIED LIFE

Teaching Career (Audio Vol. 51)

Since teaching was such a part of my life, I want to tell you about some of my experiences. I started out in fall of 1965. I had graduated in May of 1965, and we'd gotten married in June. We lived the first summer in Centerfield, and then, we moved up in the fall to Provo because Brent had one more year for his bachelor's degree. I had graduated with a Child Development and Family Relations and an Elementary Ed composite major, and so I got a teaching job in a first grade at Cherry Hill Elementary. It was a brand-new school and had just been completed. I had worked a little bit in classrooms, but to have your own class makes you really nervous. I was also nervous because my room was right by the office, so if my kids were out of control, the office would hear my class.

After you get more comfortable, you realize you can handle it. But the thing I remember about teaching is that you have a bunch of really good colleagues to work with, and without those colleagues, I would not have made it through because I had so many questions. They were so nice to me. It turned out to be a really good career start. Brent would come over at night; he had to study, so he'd bring his books over and lay on the floor in the middle of the room studying while I would put up bulletin boards.

When Brent graduated, he went into the seminary program, and we moved to Kaysville, Utah. I had just become pregnant with Doug, and I hadn't planned on teaching. We could make it on Brent's salary. One of the school board members was in our ward, and he found out I had a teaching degree and some experience teaching. So, he came up to me and asked if I'd be willing to teach because at Farmington Elementary they had more kids than they could fit into their first grade. They needed to make a new classroom on the stage and asked if I'd be willing to teach it. I said, "Well, I couldn't finish the year because I'm pregnant and due to have this baby in April, so there'd be another month of school after the baby would be born. He said it would be fine; they needed me really badly and he talked me into it.

It was quite the experience teaching on a stage with 20 students. You don't really have a door, just a curtain that separates the stage from the recreation hall where the lunchroom was. It was kind of different because lunches were very noisy and when classes would come into the gym for PE because of bad weather, the large curtain that separated our class from the gym didn't work very well in keeping out the noise. There were a lot of little things that we had to learn to deal with, among which we didn't have a bathroom close, so we had to set up times for kids to go to the bathroom. But it was one of the most fun years I had. We learned how to focus during reading and math times. Our class did well and excelled in their schoolwork. The teachers were so good to work with there as well. At the end of the year, we had a dance festival, and I remember I had to teach the first grade this dance that was just funny. I really looked like an elephant because I was about ready to have the baby. It was at the very end of the pregnancy, and I had to go in and help some of these little kids do their dance. I remember on the day of the dance performance, one little kid's partner didn't show up, so I had to dance with him out there. You can imagine and visualize this really huge teacher out there dancing with this little first-grader so they would feel comfortable doing it. But anyway, I had all these nice people come up and tell me how brave I was to do that, and the kids really enjoyed it.

Early marriage to Brent

After that year, I took a break. I decided to stay home. At school, they made other arrangements for the extra kids, so I could stay home with our new baby, and that was a great adjustment. It was hard for me for a while because I had never been a mother. I hadn't ever had siblings growing up, so it was a learning curve, but we all made it through. A couple years later, Brent got his master's degree from BYU. He traveled back and forth for a while, and then, he wanted to get a doctorate degree from Florida State. So, we moved to Tallahassee, Florida. I was pregnant again, this time with Tammy, (Tamara Sue Barlow) and we rented a Uhaul and had our old car pull it. The air conditioner in the car didn't work so we rolled down all the windows as we drove across the country in the heat. We stripped Doug down to his diaper to keep him cooler. It was before car seats so we built up the backseat so he had a flat surface to lay on. We did stop in New Orleans for a break and did some sight-seeing which was a welcome relief.

In Tallahassee, we rented a house in which two women had lived together with their dogs. There were bugs galore, so when they moved out, they let off some insect bombs. When we walked into the living room of this house, there were all these little creatures on their backs, kicking their legs. There was even a snake crawling across the floor. At that point, I decided maybe I didn't want to move to Florida. Maybe I'd like to go back home. But anyway, we survived, and Brent put up the crib. We got Doug settled in his bed, put up our bed, and just got the basics that we needed for the night. I learned that If you get up in the middle of the night, if you flip on the light, all the cockroaches scurry back to wherever they go. Oh, it was crazy. I was so paranoid that I would step on a cockroach. I made sure if I got up in the middle of the night, I would shake out my house shoes because cockroaches like to hide in dark places. One time during the night, I remember turning over in bed, and the sheet brushed my arm. I sat up in bed, screaming, and Brent… was shouting, "What's wrong?" And I said, "There's a roach on me!" But, I looked, and it wasn't a roach, just a sheet. I can still remember the feeling.

Living in that house had its advantages. It had lots of large trees all around the place. The back yard had lots of grass and plenty of room to play. . It had a long drive-way where Doug learned to coast down by himself. One day we were in our car riding down a tree covered road, and right in front of us, a huge tortoise was crossing the road. Brent stopped the car; we got the tortoise, put it in a box, and took it home. Brent drilled a small hole in its shell, and we tied a rope to it and gave it plenty of rope so it could go all over our backyard. It stayed with us quite a while before it somehow got loose and moved on.

Teaching Kindergarten in Tallahassee and Managing Apartments

Back to our story about my teaching jobs. My mom came out from Utah to watch Doug. She was living alone at the time. My dad had passed away the previous year, and she was lonely, so we invited her out and made arrangements for her in the other bedroom. I found a private school to work at, and I taught kindergarten all day. I had two aides – one was a young black mother who was an awesome worker, and the other was a male student from the university who was working to get his degree. We worked all together during the day and everything seemed to go well. We even had nap time in the afternoon where we put all the kids on cots, and they would sleep for an hour or they at least had to stay on their cots for an hour. We had a cook in our facility, and she would serve hot lunch for everybody. Having aides made the teaching more fun, especially if the aides were as good as ours. I only taught for a while because I became pregnant and my mom had to go back to Utah.

Eventually, we moved from our house into an apartment complex called Plantation Apartments. Brent maintained the yards for a while to make extra money, and we decided to move there when they offered us a management position. It had nearly 100 units, and it would pay our rent and give us a salary. Brent could go to school while I ran the apartments. I had Doug at the time and was due to have Tammy at any time. Tammy had to have a blood exchange when she was born, within 24 hours, so she stayed in the hospital for a few days. While she was in the hospital, we moved from one apartment to the manager's apartment. We lived there for a while, and I enjoyed managing the apartments. Doug, who was 2 at the time, got to know a lot of the residents, and I had to watch him closely or he would go out and visit people. One time I found him jumping up and down on the diving board outside our apartment.

Brent and I managed Plantation Apartments in Florida

Someone did not lock the pool gate when they left. I thought I would have to jump in the pool with my dress on to get Doug, but I managed to talk him down off the diving board. It was incidents such as that one that helped us decide to take out a loan and move into student housing. We had been managers for about a year, and Brent had to be in school most of the time. Neighbors would help me with the kids when I had to take care of managerial problems, but having two small children made the job more stressful.

Living in Student Housing

We were very fortunate to get into student housing. We had two bedrooms, a bathroom, kitchen, and living room. The bedrooms and bathroom were upstairs, and the kitchen and living room were on the main level. There were lots of kids near us, and we made some very good friends. As our husbands were all in graduate school, several of the wives became my good friends and we would all get together and plan activities to keep our kids busy. During our stay in student housing, we added another son, Brian (Brian Robert Barlow), to our family. When Brian was born and we took him home from the hospital, we found out he had a hernia and would need surgery. He was very unhappy and was in pain a lot until we finally got his surgery taken care of and then we found him to be a more peaceful baby.

Moving to Carbondale, Illinois

Brent finally finished his PhD and we all celebrated. Next we moved to Carbondale, Illinois where Brent got a job teaching at SIU. Doug and Tammy went to preschool there as well. We rented a house on Skyline Drive which was in a normal neighborhood. Doug and Tammy had "Big Wheels" and there was plenty of sidewalk to ride on. They loved it. Brent loved teaching there and received a Teaching Award for excellence in teaching. He also served as Counselor to the Branch President there after which he became Branch President with Scott Cowley and Bob Sturgeon as his counselors. Both families became good friends of ours. We had some neighbors who had a son, Kenny Garry, who Tammy hit it off with. They spent hours riding their Big Wheels. The Bekkers and the Clugstons lived near us and became good friends as well. We added child #4, Jon (Jonathan Warren Barlow) in Carbondale. The birth went well. The hospital provided us with a steak dinner to celebrate which was very nice.

Moving to Eau Claire, Wisconsin

After three more years, Brent got a new teaching job in Menomonie, Wisconsin. We then moved to Eau Claire, Wisconsin. We decided to live in Eau Claire because our Church had a Ward there, and we felt it was good to be close by so the kids could participate in more activities. By this time, we had Doug, Tammy, Brian, and Jon, and we were expecting Jason in November. We bought our first house in a nice neighborhood, not too far from our church.

It was on 127 East Fillmore Ave. We were near a strip mall where there was a nice grocery store, a hardware store, and a variety 5 and dime store. There were a lot of kids in the neighborhood as well. Brent had a 30 minute drive to work in Menomonie each day, but all in all, we thought we got a good deal. One different thing about Wisconsin was their yards. There were no fences in their yards, and you could see yards and yards of grass down the blocks. Brent served as a counselor in the Bishopric with Tom Miller , Bishop; and Bob Pedersen, 1st Counselor.   Two things I remember about the Eau Ward are some events that happened to us not too long after we moved there. When I was late in my pregnancy, my Ob/Gyn found a couple of growths when he was examining me; one on my ovary, and the other on my thyroid. He told me they would have to be taken out shortly after Jason was born.

About two weeks after Jason was born, I was scheduled for surgery and Sister Pederson showed up at our house. She came to take Jason for a couple weeks to let me recover from my surgery. Also, some other sisters in our ward arranged to pick up the kids from school to take them to their house until Brent got home from work. They would feed everyone dinner and then Brent would take everyone back home and put them to bed. The next morning Brent would get breakfast for the family and then drop them off at school, and the process was repeated again. Our preschoolers would be taken to someone's home to play with their kids, and Brent would pick them up after work. That was service in action!!!

Another wonderful experience that happened to me was after I had had surgery. It was the evening after my surgery and I was getting ready to go to sleep. In walked this sister from Menomonie, Sister Cagle (I can't remember if that is the right name). She had a large family with a nursing baby. After she nursed her baby, she had put her to bed and driven 30 miles over to visit me. She had her knitting with her and planned to stay the night with me. She said that in her family, someone is always there the first night after surgery in case you wake up and can't sleep and need to talk. I would doze in and out of sleep, but she would always be there to talk when I woke up. She stayed the whole night and then went back to nurse her baby about 7:00 am., driving the 30 miles back home to Menomonie. I will always remember her and that kind act. Before that, I didn't even know her, except we were sisters in the Gospel.

About this time, Brent's mom who had cancer passed away and Doug and Brent went out to the funeral, but we still stayed there. He was teaching in Menomonie Wisconsin while we lived there. One funny thing about the neighbors is they couldn't understand why we were having our fifth child; I mean they had two or three and they kept saying, Why would you want another child? '' I said, " I kind of like children."

Moving back to Utah

We went back to Utah because after the death of his wife, Brent's Dad was not doing so well. He was lonely and having a hard time adjusting. We applied to several places in Utah, and Brent got a job at BYU. We moved back there and found a house to live in,

Faculty picture at Manila Elementary

but it needed a lot of work. The house was owned by Verl and Kris Osmond. Verl's brother Tom and his wife Lynn lived next door. We lived there for a few years, and then, the expenses started to build. As the kids got older, we started to encounter more bills, for things like braces. After I had Kristin, we decided that I'd better recertify for teaching. I got free tuition because of Brent teaching at BYU, so I didn't have to pay for it, and I did it all in one summer. Then, I applied for a part-time job because all the kids were going back to school. I thought that would be good because I'd be home by the time they got home from school, and it seemed to work out well.

I taught for a year or two before I got pregnant with Brandon. By the time Brandon was born, I started to look for a part-time position so I could be home when the kids got home from school. We needed the money, and it was a blessing my mom was in good health; so she watched Brandon. I first taught at Barratt Elementary in American Fork. They had a lot of kindergarteners that year, so they made a small classroom in the paint room between two kindergarten classes. There were no doors; it was all open. I had about 18 students I taught in that middle paint room. They put three tables up with six kids at each table. There wasn't much room between the countertops with the tables in the middle, and we had to be really quiet because there were classes on either side of us.

We could hear them teaching, so it was kind of awkward, but we managed. We did a lot of fun things and were very creative. Sometimes, we would go outside if the weather was nice. Anyway, we got through it and it turned out to be a good experience. But the next year, they had a decrease in enrollment and didn't need another teacher. So I had to find another position. It just so happened that they were

Me as Cat in the Hat at Halloween in 1st Grade

opening up a brand new school in Pleasant Grove.

The new school, Manila Elementary, wasn't far from Barratt. It wasn't open for the first part of the school year, but they transferred kids from other schools to Manila once we started after the Christmas break. At that time, the outside playgrounds were not yet installed and you had to have recess inside in the gym during the winter months. Finally when the weather got better, they put sidewalks and blacktop in, even playground equipment and a ball diamond, but to begin with, it was a mess.

This was the first time I had a regular classroom to myself since I started teaching. I first just taught part-time in the mornings, and my mom watched Brandon. Donna Gurney was the only other kindergarten teacher. She taught full-time. After a few years, Sandra Bell was hired as another full-time teacher. We had a storage room between us that

Teaching award Alpine School District while at Manila

we shared. We three taught several years together and became really good friends. I still taught half-time, and they were both full-time. I taught half-time for a long time until the enrollment went up in Manila. At first, I talked the principal into allowing me to teach half-time still because I didn't want to be away from home. I shared the job with another lady whose name was Kathy Whitehead. She was really easy-going, and we worked well together. I was very blessed in the people that I worked with. Eventually, Kathy transferred to a different school, and I taught full-time there. Doug was planning to go on a mission. We had all these expenses, so I decided to go full-time, and it worked out well.

During my time at Manila, I developed a reading homework program for the kindergarten students. It turned out to be really, really successful, and all of the parents wanted to participate in it. It became really awkward because I was doing it in my room, and all the kids wanted to do it. So, the parents were complaining to Mrs. Gurney because they wanted the same program that I was doing in my classroom. I went to Donna and said, "I can give you everything if you want to." I didn't make any of the kids do it. It just started because I felt some kids needed more of a challenge than they were getting in school, and they really wanted t o read. The parents were behind it, so she started it as well, and we kind of did it together.

On my 70th birthday, she wrote in this book she gave me about how she used the program, even after moving to Vineyard Elementary. Even though she retired, she trained the other teachers, and they used my program. So, it turned out that it was kind of beneficial, and it helped the kids so much.

The other thing was we had to do a program every year, our principal was about getting kids involved at an early age. I did approve, and the parents loved the programs, and so he'd have every grade level do a program every year. I started writing the programs for this, and they were kind of simple at first but got better as we went. We'd collaborate with the other two teachers and come up with these programs. We had every kind of program there ever was, and it was really kind of a big headache, but it turned out well.

In my teaching experience, the thing that I loved about kindergarten and first grade was the excitement the kids had when they learned to read or when they finally understood something new they were struggling with. You could see that "A-ha!" moment in their eyes, and they were so excited. That thrill is just so wonderful. I mean, it will make your day. And so, when that happened, the kids did so well, and they loved coming into school each day. That made teaching worthwhile, and it made teaching a passion of mine that I don't regret at all. For teaching all those years and all those experiences I had, I will be eternally grateful.

CHAPTER 8: BEING A WIFE AND MOTHER

Being a Mother (Audio Vol. 22)

Now, I want to talk about something I hope I don't get too emotional about, and this is about being a mother. We have seven children – some were born in Utah and some were born in other states where we were living at the time. I wanted to talk not about going through the pain part of birth, but the part that I felt about each child, the night after they were born, and after everybody else had gone home. People would always come up to see our baby shortly after I gave birth, and then, I was left alone with a baby in my room which was such an emotional time for me.

Early married with Doug and Tammy

Doug's birth was kind of a funny thing. I was teaching up to about a week before he was born, and my mom and dad came up from California early because they wanted to be there for the birth of their first grandson. They were living at our house, and my dad was very anxious. Every day, he'd say, "Well, when are you gonna go and have that baby?" And I would say, "Well, it's not up to me, it's up to the baby." I was having contractions one day, and I called the doctor and went down because he wanted to check me. His wife was going to have a baby as well, and so we had to go over to Bountiful Hospital. We were living in Kaysville at the time and there wasn't a hospital in Kaysville. And so, he says, "Well, I'll be over at the hospital because we had to induce my wife, and she might have the baby tonight." I was having contractions already, but he thought I might take a long time having it because it was my first baby.

He told me to come over to the hospital where I would feel more comfortable and said it would probably take me all night and maybe part of the next day to have the baby. I went home and told the family what I was going to do. Brent would take me over to the hospital, but nobody else needed to come because the doctor said it might be a long time. So, we went over and got checked into the hospital. They prepped me and left me alone in the room. The minute that they left me in the room I started having these really hard contractions. I remember getting really nauseous, and so I rang for the nurse who then came and checked me, and she said, "Oh you're ready to deliver." The doctor had just come out of the room from being with his wife who had just delivered their baby. At this point, I didn't have any medication or anything. I had agreed to have an epidural, or at that time, they gave a paracervical that kind of blocks the lower part of your body. So, they medicated me, and I was ready. The baby was starting to come, and so they took me in, and I had Doug. I couldn't feel it; it was really a good birth as far as pain goes because after he gave me the block, I had no more pain. I could just feel the pressure.

Doug's Birth (Audio Vol. 22)

When Doug was born, he came out and was really blue. He wasn't getting enough oxygen, so they put oxygen on him, and then, he started crying and turned pink. I remember thinking, "Oh this was such a wonderful thing!" It was around 9:30 or 10 at night when he was born, so Brent stayed a while before he went back home, and I was there with the baby alone. They brought the baby into me and just let me hold him. I got to thinking about what a miracle it was to have this little, tiny baby. I took the blanket off and looked at his toes and his fingers. I was so grateful for this opportunity to become a mom. I remember at that point, I prayed to Heavenly father. I was so thankful that I was blessed to become a mom and to have this opportunity to have children. It is such a miracle that this happened. With Doug and every single child, I had different experiences, but I never felt as close to Heavenly Father as I did when I gave birth. And Doug was the very first.

One time, when Doug was older, I was across the street, and there was a guy that had this fancy sports car, and we caught the kids over there putting rocks in his gas tank, (or so we thought). We had to contact the guy, and he was really, really upset. We thought they had opened the gas cap and put rocks in, so we had to have someone take apart the gas tank to make sure we didn't ruin his car. It turned out that no rocks had gotten into the tank.

Tammy's Birth (Audio Vol. 23)

Tammy was our second. I was pregnant with her when we went to Florida, and Brent was working towards his PhD down there. I worked all the time while I was pregnant with her. I taught a private school kindergarten class, and my mom came down to take care of Doug.

Tammy's birth was in Florida, and when she was born, she had a blood incompatibility. She was really jaundiced and within 24 hours, her Bilirubin count spiked really high. They were worried that if we went another night that it might get too high. If it goes too high, it causes brain damage. So, they did a blood exchange. I don't understand totally how they do it, but they take a lot of her blood out and replace it with fresh blood, and somehow the body makes new blood. It was like she kind of had a fresh start. She had to do this within 24 hours of her birth, and when I went home from the hospital, I pumped breast milk for a while, and they fed it to her in the hospital. While she was in the hospital, we took over the management of Plantation Apartments, so we had to move to the new manager's apartment. I would go back and forth from the hospital to feed her while we moved all our stuff.

When I finally brought her home from the hospital, we didn't even have the crib set up, so I made a bed in a drawer and put some blankets down. I would feed her, then put her in the drawer where she slept. (Don't worry, I DIDN'T shut the drawer!!!) She was so awesome to do that. I got everything moved from the other apartment, cleaned the other apartment, and then, I organized the new apartment so it would function as an office and a living space for our family so Brent could go to school. I ran the apartments, and it worked well. We had really good neighbors that helped with this. I would get the baby to sleep, and a neighbor would come over and listen while I'd go work.

So, that was the beginning of Tammy's life. She was an awesome baby, and it was so fun to have a little girl because now we had a little boy and a little girl. Being in the apartments was great. Doug, however, could be a problem there. He liked to go visit all the people in the apartments. We had some apartments that were all men, all boys, or students, and there were some that were married couples. But, the guys took a liking to Doug, and he would go up and knock on their door, and they would invite him in. I would get so mad because then I'd have to go around and search where he was. They taught him how to play cards and did all these things with Doug. He was so friendly. One time, somebody left the gate of the pool open, which was outside our apartment, and he went inside the gate and got on the diving board. He was jumping up and down on the diving board, when I looked out my front window and saw him out there. I had a dress on, and I had to go out there and say, "Doug, you need to turn around and walk down and get off the diving board. You are not supposed to be in here, it's very dangerous. You don't know how to swim, yet." I didn't know if I would have to go jump in the water to get Doug out, but I managed to talk him down. After that, I would lock the door so he would not ever go out until I was with him. It was interesting seeing his life start that way, but Tammy was such a good baby through it all. She was wonderful to have, and we just had experience after experience of great times with both Doug and Tammy.

Brian's Birth (Audio Vol. 24)

Brian's birth . At this point, we had managed the apartments for a couple of years, and we decided that it was too stressful. We just wanted to get through school and get out of there, so Brent decided to go full-time. We applied for student housing and moved over to university housing. We had a townhouse there with two bedrooms upstairs and a kitchen/ living room combination downstairs.

I remember when we had Brian, his doctor was a real cowboy. He wore cowboy boots in the room where I had the baby. He was kind of a laid-back doctor, but I really liked him. He was in a group with four other doctors, but he's the one that I had when I gave birth to Brian. Brian took a little bit longer with the delivery because he was posterior. You have to realize that when we were out of Utah, the pain management system for babies was different. In Florida, you could choose either to have gas which knocks you out, or you could have nothing. They didn't have epidurals or anything to cut the pain, and I wanted to be awake for my babies to be born.

I wanted to be brave, but when he had to go in, he had to go in with his hands and turn Brian so that he could be born. The doctor said, ``Do you want me to put you out or it'll only take a minute for me to turn him. So, he went in with his hands and turned Brian around. It was the worst thing ever, but we made it through. Brian was born, and he was healthy, cute, and so lovable. Also, the hospital back then would give you a steak dinner when you had a baby, and you and your husband could have some alone time together, complete with music, candlelight and wine (which I saved for our neighbors).

We went home to the apartment, and Brian began having problems crying like he was in pain. He would go to sleep, then if he turned a little bit the wrong way, he would start crying again. So, I took him to the doctor, and we found out he had a hernia. They were going to have to operate. They scheduled the surgery for the next day, so I took him home. That was the worst night ever. He never stopped crying all night. I would sit in the rocking chair and prop pillows all around in case I fell asleep, so he wouldn't fall out of my arms on the floor. The only time he would sleep is when I held him a certain way, and it would push on that hernia so he could get relief. He would immediately fall asleep. Well, that night, that's what I had to do. We took him to the doctor the next day because he started crying really hard again, and the doctor had to work really hard to get the hernia back in, so he decided to check him into the hospital and do the surgery then. The surgery went well and the next day we were able to take him home. His life was so much better after that, and he was a much happier baby.

Jon's Birth (Audio Vol. 25)

Now, for the story of Jon's birth. In the meantime, Brent had gotten his PhD from Florida State, and we got our first job in Carbondale, Illinois at Southern Illinois University (SIU). Brent got a teaching job there, and we rented a house on Skyline Drive which is where we lived when we had Jon. I went to an OBGYN that was in a practice with three other doctors, and the rumor was that one of the doctors had a drinking problem. So, I swore that I would not go to that doctor when Jon was ready to be born. I would wait until another doctor went on call. But, of course, you know that never happens the way you want it to. And so, this doctor was on call that day. He was really nice. I would study him to see if I could figure out if he was drinking or not, but the birth went fine. Jon was born, and he was healthy. He had blue eyes and blonde hair from the get-go. I looked at him and said, "Where did he come from?" All of our kids had dark hair and dark eyes, and Jon was just so different, but it was so fun to have a little blond-haired, blue-eyed boy. He was even-tempered, and he was a great baby. We survived having this doctor deliver him, and this hospital also gave us a fancy dinner with all the trimmings. We had a good time in Illinois while we lived there. It was a great neighborhood.

Brent became the branch president for a while there, and we gained a lot of friends. We had good experiences there. Brent loved teaching at SIU and he received an Outstanding Teacher Award there. He was an excellent teacher, and his students loved him. He did much good for the community as well.

Doug was in first grade there and had a black teacher named Mrs. Perkins. She became his favorite teacher and was exceptionally good at Math, and Doug loved her. She taught him to add in base 2.

Jason's Birth (Audio Vol. 26)

When we moved to Wisconsin, I was pregnant with Jason. Brent's new job was at University of Wisconsin-Stout in Menomonie, Wisconsin, about 30 miles from Eau Claire. Our church was in Eau Claire. At that time, primary and Relief Society were held during the week, and we felt like we needed to live in Eau Claire so the kids could participate in all the activities.   It would be easier to have Brent travel than me with the kids.

Both Eau Claire and Menomonie were beautiful. We bought our first house in Eau Claire for $27,000. In Wisconsin, they don't have fences in the backyard; we just had beautiful green lawns that go as far as you can see down the backyards. And so, it was kind of a new experience, and we got to know our neighbors very well. We had, by this time, Doug, Tammy, Brian, and Jon – four kids total. I was pregnant with Jason, who would be our fifth, and my neighbors who became our really good friends said, "Why would you want to have a fifth child?" I told them that we liked children and wanted a large family.   They couldn't believe it because most everybody had two, maybe three at the most.

I found a good doctor after asking neighbors and people at church for recommen-dations. My doctor was from Taiwan. He only had two children, and he asked me why I wanted a fifth child. But, he was so nice, and he was very thorough. I had a really good relationship with him, and I was really glad somebody had recommended him. In fact, when I was pregnant and going to visit him for well visits, he found that I had a lump on my thyroid and a lump on my ovary that would have to be surgically removed. They did not want to do it until after I had Jason.   It didn't cause pain or anything, but the doctor said they should be removed. And so I knew I had that surgery to look forward to.

The birth of Jason was unique, and we all think Jason's kind of a laid-back guy because of his birth. When Jason was born, I didn't have any pain medicine. It was all natural, and when I was dilated to 10, the nurses wheeled me into the birthing room. They told me not to push because the doctor wasn't there yet. That was the worst part. The birthing room had the lights dimmed low. They had music playing softly, and they had this big tub next to the table where I was. The water in the tub was body tempera-ture. Everything was calm, and everybody talked in soft voices. When the doctor came in, I proceeded to have Jason. I remember it wasn't too hard – he came in just a couple of pushes. I was really ready to have him, but when he came out, the cord was wrapped around his neck. The doctor was really stressed and had to cut the cord around his neck, and Jason started screaming. They put him on my stomach and said to massage his back, and so we did that. Then, when he calmed down a bit, the doctor took him and gave him to Brent who slowly lowered him into the water. When he hit that water, he just relaxed and spread his arms and legs out. He looked around at the lights and everything, and he was so peaceful that they let him stay there for a few minutes. Then, they laid him into a heated blanket and wrapped it around him.

They let me hold him, and he was the most relaxed baby I've ever seen. That's what I remember most about Jason. He had the calmest delivery after being traumatized at first because of the cord; then he just relaxed. And so, we always say Jason's kind of a laid-back guy. That's what he is, but I think it's because of how he was born.

We brought him home from the hospital.   After we were home for about a week, the doctor told me I needed to go back in and have that surgery. I had a new baby and four other children. The ward there was so wonderful. Everybody came and offered to watch the kids. We made a plan. Brent went into work a little bit late. He got all the kids ready in the morning for school, and the youngest one, which was Jon, went over to sister Pederson's house with the baby. She kept the baby all night and day while I was in the hospital. Then, when Brent got home from work, he would just pick up the other kids from neighbors or friends and bring them home. The ward was awesome. They would bring food over every night, their kids would play with our kids, and it wasn't traumatic for anyone during that time. When I came home from the hospital, the Pedersons even kept Jason for a little longer until I'd had a couple of days to rest. When I took over, I couldn't lift him, so he spent a lot of time in his bassinet while I gained strength and got back to normal. That's how we started off, and it was really good. We loved living in the ward. We lived there for about three years before we moved to Utah again.

Kristen's Birth (Audio Vol. 28)

Brent's mom passed away while we were living in Eau Claire. Doug and Brent went out to her funeral. She had cancer and was really sick. After her death, Brent's dad was so sad and wasn't doing well. So we made a decision to find a job and move back to Utah and be there for his dad.

At this point in my life, I was the healthiest I had been in a long time. I had lost weight. I was running three miles a day with my friend Carol Webber. She and I would run together every morning by State Street on Eighth North, and we were both on Weight Watchers. I was really healthy, and I didn't know that I was pregnant. When I was about three months pregnant, I miscarried. They said it was not anything I did, it just happened. I was really upset about that because it was the first miscarriage I'd ever had. We survived it and everything, and I felt okay, but I was just worried and decided that I was too healthy.

I got pregnant again, but this time, I was a little heavier, and I wasn't running three miles a day. I carried the baby fine. So, I thought maybe my body doesn't do that well if I'm really healthy. So anyway, I became pregnant. They didn't usually tell what the sex of the baby was, or they would guess from different things like its heart rate. They said, "Oh it could be a girl or could be a boy." Well, we had one girl and four boys at this point, and so I thought another girl would be nice to round out the family. But I didn't dare hope because I thought for sure that Jason and Jon would be girls.

I was healthy through the pregnancy. I remember at the time when I was ready to deliver, I'd had contractions during the night, so Brent stayed home for part of the morning, and we were kind of watching to see if we should go to the hospital or not. Eventually, it stopped, and I didn't have any contractions. I thought it was probably a false alarm. Brent decided to run to the mall really quickly to grab something. We didn't have cell phones back then. He'd gone to the mall, and I didn't know how to reach him. He called back once to check on me, but I was fine at the time. Then, I started having contractions one on top of another. I was about ready to go find a neighbor who was there to run me to the hospital because he wasn't home yet. When he pulled into the driveway, I was walking around outside, all packed and ready to go. I threw the suitcase in the car and told him we needed to go now. We got there just in time, and I had time for an epidural, so they gave me an epidural. That was such a nice thing to have after all those births I'd gone through with nothing. The epidural was like heaven.

I had Kristen, and the neighborhood put a big banner up when I brought her home from the hospital. They gave me all these cute baby clothes with little dresses and things like this because I had tons of boys' clothes, but I didn't have very many girls' clothes. She was a wonderful addition to our family, and we lived at this house for quite a while. Then, we decided that we had saved some money and would try building a house. We looked around and found a lot to build on, just a few blocks away, and we built the new house and put our house up for sale. It did not sell for a long time, and we decided if it wouldn't sell, then we would rent it out.

Brandon's Birth (Audio Vol. 29)

We had Brandon at the 666 house before we moved to our new house. Brandon was born with his feet turned inward, and so we knew that we had to do something for him. He was healthy other than that, but babies' bones are more movable when they are very young and when they get older, their bones get hard. So, I took him to a pediatrician, and he thought we should put shoes on him at night. You put a bar between the shoes, and you have to screw them together, and it makes it so that he can't move his feet. This was not good because first of all, I was 41 years old and teaching school. Brandon cried all night long. It was so uncomfortable for him that he couldn't stand it. Imagine if your feet are kept in one place and you can't move them. It would be so frustrating, and a baby wouldn't know what was going on.

So, I took him back to the pediatrician and said, "We can't do this. I can't sleep, and he can't sleep. We're all miserable. So, is there another option?" And he said we could cast his feet and legs and bring him in every week for a new cast. We did this, and he was so much better because he could move his legs and feet, even though it was heavier. We had a big laundry tub in our house, so I'd come home from work in the afternoon and stand him in the wash tub so the cast would become soft and I could unwind it. Then, I would bathe him and take him back to the pediatrician, and he would put new casts on his legs.

We did this for about a year of his life, and he even stood up and started to walk on the casts because he was used to them. Most of the clothes that Brandon wore when he was little was a shirt and a diaper because you couldn't get his pants up over both casts. He learned to walk around the furniture with casts on, and he was a much happier baby doing that than with the special shoes bolted together. His legs grew strong and well-formed. He didn't have any deformity in his legs and was able to walk and run, so that was worth everything.

How Our Children Got Their Names (Audio Vol. 42)

First of all, we could never decide on names for our children until they were born because I felt we had to look at the child, and the child had to fit the name. So, with Doug, Brent's mom and dad had certain rules. They wanted his name to be after his dad. My husband's dad's name is Alvin Robert Barlow, and I just couldn't bring myself to name him Alvin. I kept thinking of the chipmunks. Then, my mom and dad had certain ideas too. They wanted Cecil, which was my dad's name, and I couldn't bring myself to name Doug Cecil, even for a middle name. Well, we found a name that nobody even mentioned, and so that's where Doug came from. His middle name is Brent, Douglas Brent. But, I felt good about that. I didn't want him named Brent as his first name because then we would get the two Brents mixed up. We both liked it. It was not a revelation or anything, it was just kind of a matter of Okay, what was left that nobody liked or voiced their opinion on.

Now, Tammy's name is Tamara Sue Barlow, which was obviously after me, her mom. Tammy was named because Brent was doing some research on Jeremiah, and Tamera was the Queen in Ireland. Her name was probably related to the Ark of the Covenant that he was studying. I thought the name Tamera was kind of pretty, but it was kind of old. So, we made it Tamara and there was not anybody named Tamara around then. Then, it became really popular after we named her. But, Tamara doesn't go by Tamara, she goes by Tammy which fits her better. She doesn't look like a Tamara; she looks more like a Tammy, and that's how she got her name.

I can't remember where we got Brian. We just liked the name Brian. It's not a big thing. Robert is his middle name, and that was after Grandpa Barlow's middle name, Alvin Robert Barlow.

Our next child we named him Jonathan. I liked the name but I thought the name was too long. I considered renaming him just Jon. I like the name Jonathan, but I really never called any of our kids anything more than one syllable. When you have seven kids and you have to call their names, it's easier to say one syllable. And so, we call him Jon and we gave him his middle name Warren after my Grandpa. I told him he was probably the most peaceful child we had, and thought he had the right personality to get through to my grandpa because my grandpa was kind of stubborn. His name was Warren Claire Day. I think deep in my grandpa's soul he was a good man, and he had a good heart. I hoped that he would see reason and join the church on the other side because we did his work for him and his wife. Grandpa and I grew really close, even though we argued a lot, but I have good feelings for my grandpa.

Next is Jason. I don't know where his name came from. I kind of liked Jason Todd Barlow. They said, "Well did you get it from something historical or from family history or something?" I said "No, really our good friends the Bekkers had a son named Todd Bekker." Our kids would play together and ride bikes and I liked the name. So, it's not that it was a super person or anything, I just liked the name. And so, that's where Jason Todd came from.

After Jason was Kristin, and I really don't know where Kristin came from, but Elizabeth was my mom's middle name, and there are a lot of Elizabeth's on both sides of our family tree, either as a middle name or a first name. So, I thought Elizabeth was a name that fits Kristin. As the rule is, I tend to call her Kris, but anyway, Kristen fits her too.

Brandon was the tail-end, and I don't know why I liked Brandon either. Brandon and James were people in our family tree that I would see when I would look through for names. So that worked out really well. And I hope my kids like their names. They seem to fit them. Names stay with you for eternity, so I guess we'd better like them.

Church Callings and Experiences (Audio Vol. 52)

I've had a variety of church callings. . First of all, I started even when I was in high school. I took piano lessons and got called to play the piano for primary. Sometimes, I got to be the chorister. I did play the piano for the missionaries also when they'd have a baptism. I learned five or six songs really well. When we had songs for the baptism, I said they had to choose one of those songs if they wanted it played well. I went through first and thought the songs would talk about baptism or making your life better. Those are the callings I started with in high school.

When I was in college, I taught some teaching classes in Sunday school because they didn't have Primary. Sometimes, I would be on committees with the Relief Society and so I kind of did various things. When I got married and was out of college, I worked in Primary mostly at first. usually teaching younger kids up to about 10 in primary, and then, I was called into Young Women. I was a counselor and an advisor, which included helping out with camp activities. I've also been in Relief Society as a counselor several times as well as a Relief Society President a couple of times, but every single thing I did in each of these callings were a little bit different.

Every calling you have, you learn something new from it. You probably do a little more in the mission field. You find out that maybe you're the primary chorister as well as a teacher in Sunday School or Primary because there are not as many people who can serve. That's a real benefit in the mission field because you get a lot of experience, and it's kind of everybody working together to make it work, and it did well for us. For instance, so far in young women I've learned I had Beehives first as an advisor and then I was a counselor in the Young Women Presidency over the Beehives. The great thing that I loved about it was the girls; the service projects and other activities were so good and so rewarding. You get to know the girls and feel like you made a difference in their lives.

I remember as a youth I had the same experience with leaders that I had. It wasn't called Young Women, but it was called Mutual back then, but it was the same kind of thing. And so, I think it's really a divine thing that this is a calling to help youth who need good guidance. In primary, I was mainly a teacher, and I got to be a secretary at one time. And the funny thing about being the secretary, they had a couple of autistic kids in our class who were very disruptive, so they sat them back by me. One kid, I remember, did paper-folding all the time, but then, sometimes I'd ask him. He would hear what people were talking about in class, but he could not sit still without doing something else. Being a secretary is fun, I think it's kind of a cushy job, in that you do records, but you get around, and you have a little freedom in what you do. Nursery coordinator was another good calling I had. It's a whole different thing. You get to bring treats every week, and you make sure they have a short lesson. They sing a lot, and you do all these fun activities and give them a good first experience in being in a class on a modified scale.

Relief Society is the one that I want to focus on. They would say I am the first counselor, but I'm an educational counselor even though I don't think they call it that anymore. It's good because I do more reading because I get to choose all the lessons from conference talks. But the thing about it is, contact with people increases your own testimony. You learn the hard things that people have had to go through, and you realize that you're important because you're a person that cares about another person, and that's kind of what the gospel is all about. You kind of meet the needs of those around you. It can be a phone call or a stop by. it's kind of just getting them to a better place than where they were and making sure you're there for them when they need something. Helping sisters minister to make sure people have someone in their life that cares about them is key. I think those are the most important things. And it doesn't matter what your calling is in the church, you learn from that, you become a better person from it, and you hopefully can be a good influence on those that you work with.

We had lived in Wisconsin almost three years and Brent's mom passed away. They were living in Utah at the time. She had cancer and had had it for a while. She had been undergoing chemotherapy but she did not do well and was sick all the time. She passed away at home. Brent wanted to go out for the funeral, and Doug was our oldest, so he took Doug with him. I couldn't travel because I had a new baby and just had surgery, so I stayed home with the rest of the kids while Doug and Brent went out to the funeral. While life got somewhat back to normal for us, Brent's Dad wasn't doing too well. Brent's sister Jane visited him often, but he had always been closer to Brent and we knew that we probably should move back to be closer to him. And so, Brent applied for jobs in Utah, and he got a job teaching at BYU. We moved back there and found a house. We sold our old house and didn't even hardly have to list it. Some family was moving out from Utah that was LDS from Utah, and they were coming to teach at the University there. They had two or three kids, and they loved our house and bought it from us. Our neighbor used to joke when she watched as we would load our food storage onto the moving van and then watch the new tenants move their food storage off their moving van and move it into the house. She'd say, "What is this thing with Mormons? You take wheat off of one moving van, and you put wheat on another moving van, then why don't you just exchange wheat?" So, everyone had a good laugh.

We went to Utah. Brent drove with the kids, and I flew with Jason. Brent did a scenic drive with the kids, and they stopped at all these places along the way and had a great time on the journey . We stayed for a while with Brent's Dad. He was going to sell his house while we were looking to find a house in Orem. We found one there, but houses in Orem were more expensive than they were in Wisconsin. So, for what we had gotten from our house, there was nothing in that range, so we knew we had to borrow more money and get

Our Orem house at 666 N. 1000 E.

another less expensive house. Well, the only one that we could find that we thought we could manage was one with the address of 666 North, 1000 East. My husband called it "The Devil house" because of the house number 666. It turned out to be really good. It was owned by Virl Osmond, and they didn't have much money. I would think they would, being an Osmond. They had not even planted a lawn. They planted corn where their lawn should be and a garden all around it. In the house, they had only finished the upper level which had three bedrooms, the living room, and the kitchen. The third level was a four-way split with orange carpet. It had a bedroom, quite a large bedroom where we put two sets of bunks, and it had a laundry area which was partially finished. There was also a fourth level on the bottom level that was not finished at all. I remember we got it for $45,000 and that was supposed to be a real deal, but it had a lot of work that we had to do on it. Brent and I finished the basement; we learned a lot about how to do that, and then we hired people for some things that we didn't know how to do, and we got it all done.

Some funny things happened in that house. The kids had gerbils, and the gerbils had a plastic cage. At night, when everything was quiet, they were awake running in their little wheel since they are nocturnal creatures. And since the cage was plastic, they would eat it, so they would chew on the plastic and break it off until there was a hole in the plastic in the cage. We didn't know they were doing that, and they would get out of the cage. One night, Brent was reading the newspaper, and I was reading a book in the master bedroom, and out of the corner of my eye, I saw something move out of the corner of my eye. I took my book down and looked, and I saw it again because it ran around the other way. It was one of those gerbils. I jumped up on the bed and started screaming. . I took a towel and closed the door, and we put towels under the door, so it couldn't get out of that room. Then, I took another towel and threw it on top of the gerbil and grabbed it. Needless to say, we didn't buy another plastic cage to house those gerbils.

Another gerbil story. One of the other gerbils got out and got into the laundry room. There was no wall board up yet, just the insulation. This gerbil got inside the wall and went around in the insulation. It stayed in there and died because it couldn't get out. After a while, you could smell this weird, horrible smell because of this gerbil. Anyway, we took care of that, and eventually, I can't remember what happened with the gerbils, but we didn't have them for very long. After all this happened, we decided to get a different pet.

Our House at 1111 East 1045 North

When we moved over to our new house at 1111 East 1045 North, Brandon was a

Our Orem house at 1111 E. 1045 N.

young baby with casts on. We still had our house on 666 North 1000 East. So we were trying to come up with two mortgage payments a month. The lady that was renting our house had a hard time paying her rent. She and her husband were in the process of getting a divorce. She would plead her case each time she would bring over the rent. Finally, we decided it would be better if she found another place that she could afford. So after she had moved out, we decided to put a little money into the house before we listed it again.

That turned out to be a good call. We recarpeted, painted, and put in a new dishwasher. It did the trick because as soon as we listed it again, we had 5 offers. It was such a relief having just one mortgage payment.

One new addition we had at our new address was an intercom which went to all three floors. It was a fun thing in that we could put a conference on it, and you could listen to it, especially on Saturday sessions wherever you were in the house. One caution was that sometimes certain boys in the basement would want to have family prayer over the intercom which to me seemed a little sacrilegious and a little lazy!

Another addition we had at our new house was our cat Lucky. He was just a kitten that would hang around our house when it was in the construction stage so we adopted him. He loved to come into the house, except when Brent was home. Brent would shove him outside with his foot when he tried to get in. We called him "Lucky to be Alive". That name stuck when he got hit by a car and ran to our window well to heal. We finally lost him when one of the Overlys hit him when they entered our cul-de-sac driving too fast.

There were some funny things too that happened at this house! Read on:

Mom's Foot Glued to Floor (Audio Vol. 17)

I think it's time we go into some of the funny things that happened in Orem. This one, I didn't think was so funny, but the family thought it was hilarious. This happened

60

in our kitchen in Orem; We had a vinyl floor in our kitchen. Somebody had been doing some craft project using super glue, and they had left the lid off of it and left the tube on the table. It was kind of hanging over the edge of the table, and the glue had dripped onto the floor. A lot of times, I just ran around barefoot, and I was just doing some cleaning up around the kitchen so I was wiping off the table, and I started to turn around and go back, but I couldn't get my foot off the floor.

My foot was glued to the floor. I'd pull on it, and it would start to pull my skin off. Everybody was saying, "What's wrong, Mom?" And I said, "My foot is glued to the floor." Everybody started laughing, and I said "It's not funny. I cannot get my foot off the floor." They could not stop laughing. It was so terrible, and I was kind of crying and laughing because I was so frustrated, and nobody was helping me. So finally, somebody brought me a knife and I remember how everybody thought it was so funny, and they couldn't stop laughing, I thought they were so inconsiderate.

Relationships with Children (Audio Vol. 41)

So, I take this to be an overall kind of philosophy about raising children. I had a major in CDFR, or child development and family relations, and you learn about different aspects of it. Also, being a kindergarten and first grade teacher has made me aware of different personalities and behavior differences of children. Also, I'm married to a person who did counseling and was a marriage counselor, and he taught marriage. He has a lot of opinions as well, but my philosophy is built on gut feelings and experiences with life and family. My philosophy, first of all, when I first had Doug was, " Okay let's just survive," because Doug was kind of a stubborn little toad, and he would really stress me out or test the limits of my patience. I kind of learned along the way what worked and what did not work. Every one of my kids, I would think, brought out some kind of maternal thing in me, and each one was a little different. I, first of all, believe the most important thing is to develop a relationship with your child.

Of course, you need to have rules. And Brent has a saying about relationships without rules brings chaos and rules without relationships brings rebellion. I remember that, but he'll probably tell you as well, but I remember it's true. You have to have rules, and you have to have consequences for breaking the rules, but there's certain ways to do it. And I think developing a relationship is important. It's important that you can talk to your kids without losing your cool because once you lose it, it really doesn't mean anything. They kind of tune out and don't listen to you, and they just stomp off and your moment is gone.

Believe me, I've done all these things. I've learned through the years the best way is number one to have a relationship with your child and treat them as a person, more so than just as a child because they all have opinions and reasons for their opinions. They all think you're way off base and unfair, so you really need to get their opinions and understand why they feel this way. Then, it's best to get kind of a consensus of opinion and let them understand what the consequence is for what they've done and why you've come to that conclusion. I used to think, "Okay, you're the parent. You need to do it this way." But I think kids do better if they understand the why behind it. I would say also if you have a relationship with your child, you enjoy it much more. You do things with your children that build memories, and you will have a lot of time that you laugh together, and I think all of these things help make your relationship last forever.

Mom Memories of Trips (Audio Vol. 56)

Now, I'd like to talk about trips I had as a youth. When I was growing up, my dad worked for the Southern Pacific Railroad, and as a result, he could get a discount for us to ride on the trains. And so, every year, since my mom's family was from Utah, we would get to ride on the train overnight and sleep in a berth. A berth is part of the ceiling; the porter would come in and unlock it, and it would fall down, and there would be a bed. It was so fun because I remember, it had a net thing on the side that you could put your clothing in, and the bed would sleep really well because of the motion of the train. I remember my mom would always make us lunch and snacks to eat on the way, and it was a real treat because we'd wake up the next morning, get ready, and go to the dining car to order our breakfast. This was a real treat. They have porters who wore white coats, and most of the porters would be black or African American. I got to be really good friends with them, and they would bring me little decks of cards and different things during the day to keep me entertained. Sometimes after they got their work done, they would play cards with me. But anyway, that was a real fun thing going to Utah every year, and we looked forward to riding on the train. It would go to Salt Lake, and then, some of my mom's relatives would pick us up from the train, and we would usually go down and stay in Lehi.

After Brent and I got married, I remember some of the trips that we had. I remember that Brent used to speak with "Know Your Religion" and one of the places he would go a lot to was Southern California. So, every year when he would do this, he would go to a couple of areas down there, and the church would give him a stipend that would pay his expenses. He would get a fee for doing the lecture, and then, they would also give him a travel allowance and a food allowance. We would pile all the kids in the car, go to California, and stay in a hotel. We would eat at McDonalds or really cheap food because we had a lot of kids . We would go to Disneyland every year, and it was so fun. Then, Brent would go and speak at night to wherever he had to go speak, and I would stay with the kids at Disneyland. He would join us for the Electric Parade at the end of Disneyland, then we'd stay until close.

I can remember riding in the car without air-conditioning. We would roll the windows down. Also, we didn't have a TV in our car or any of those fun things they have today, so we had to make our own entertainment. I remember we had a tape player in the car, and we would sing all these old songs that we knew. We always sang " 99 bottles of beer on the wall" and "Tiny Bubbles". We'd have favorite songs that we would sing, as well as all the car games we'd play. It was just a really fun thing to do, and we'd have a lot of food in the car so we would snack. One of our favorites was spray cheese and crackers. We'd have to clean the car when we get back because it was so dirty from all the stuff we ate throughout the trip.

On our Disneyland trips, the kids would get tired in the afternoon and they would want to go back to the hotel to swim, so we would do that. Then, we would go back to Disneyland at night and stay until closing.

Another thing about trips, as we got older, we bought a Marriott time-share, and we would go to Newport Beach every year. When the family was small, we would get one unit there, and it would come with the main unit and two side bedrooms. We would stay there and go to Disneyland or other places around. Sometimes, we'd go to San Diego to the Wild Animal Park or Sea World or Knotts Berry Farm. We had a lot of activities that we did in Southern California, but Newport Beach was always a fun place to stay.. We've even had a family picture taken there. It was one of our best ones on the beach there, but California was a mainstay that we always went to.

We went to a few more places like Williamsburg, Virginia. A lot of the kids were somewhat small. I think we might even have had Doug married at the time we went there, but it was very hot. There were different parades that were ongoing and we got to go up and see Jamestown and a lot of historical places, and it was really fun.

Now, one other time I remember is when we took my mom with us on our vacation to Yellowstone. We rented a big RV, bought lots of food to snack on and prepare on the trip, and then piled everyone up in it and took off. We took a wheelchair for Grandma in case she needed it, but she could get around better than we thought. We went camping at Yellowstone, and I remember that some of the kids slept on top of the RV because we heard that there were bears around, and we didn't want anybody to sleep out on the ground. But, sure enough, during the night, we even had a bear visit. They mentioned in the camp that we shouldn't leave food out because it will attract bears and everything, but we could hear bears rummaging through the stuff out there. The kids stayed on top of the RV at that time, but I still remember that it was such an exciting thing. It added a lot of mystery and intrigue to the whole trip. It was a real fun vacation, and my mom loved it.

Brent, Doug, Grandma and I went to Ireland. Brent took Doug over there early.

Brent and I visited Ireland

Brent did a lot of research and stuff about where he thought the Arc at the Covenant was buried in Ireland. Doug was kind of an amateur photographer, so he went over there with him, and they took pictures of caves that were on some farmer's property. The farmers would let him go in and take pictures of all these hieroglyphics that were on the side of the caves from people that had lived in an earlier time. So, he and Doug were over there for a while, and then, my mom and I flew over on the plane. It was a long flight. My mom did really well, though.

We met in England, went up through Wales, Ireland, and a "Touch of Scotland." It was a place that was really wonderful. My mother talked about it for years with her friends of what a wonderful time we had. It was a really good experience, and it was a long trip. She'd never been out of the country, and we had a wonderful time there with her. Brent and I have been to Ireland several times though. I think this was the only one where kids got to go to Ireland. Brian might have gone too with Brent at one time, but I don't think I went when Brian went. Ireland is probably the country that we traveled to most.

Brent and I also went to Australia. He went with the government and BYU, and we went to different cities down there. He had to talk about marriage and family as a representative not only of the church but of the government. While he did that, then we would take tours and get to do other things. We went to a hockey tournament down there, and we got to go see Mama Mia on the live stage. I got to meet some teachers there, and they took me to an elementary school, and I saw exactly what they did. I remember one thing about that – it was mandatory that everybody wore hats outside because they were closer to the equator, and the sun was really, really hot, and skin cancer was a major thing in Australia. So, the kids had sunscreen on, and they had to wear hats whenever they went outside, which I thought was unusual and different from here in the United States. We went to the Indian Ocean, and I didn't know if it was the Pacific or Atlantic, but anyway, it was warm and beautiful. It was really nice. The people were so nice. I learnt that squash soup is what they call pumpkin soup. We ate in a lot of different places, and the people were just wonderful, very hospitable.

Another one of the trips that we went on was to Beijing, China. This time we took Brandon with us. It was really interesting. Brent was a representative of BYU and the government and had to talk to different people. Brandon is very adventurous, and he doesn't always follow the rules. For instance, they said, "Don't drink the water here, always drink bottled water." When we'd go out to restaurants, they would say it's good not to drink with ice in it because the ice is made from their regular water. So, we all followed the rule, except for Brandon who would always order ice in his pop. I kept telling him he was going to get sick, but he never did, of course. We had these little cards for when we went around to the different sites or shopping. On one side, it was English, and on the other side, it was Chinese or Mandarin and so it would have the characters there. It basically said where we wanted to go, and we had one for the hotel, so we felt really good. We could go anywhere we wanted. We went shopping at the Silk Alley, and Brandon got a whole bunch of deals that he came back and sold on the internet. But it was really kind of fun. It's kind of fun bargaining. Brent and I had a great time there.

There was another couple that went with us, and her husband was involved in speaking too. So, she went with us, and we just had a ball going all over the town and shopping and everything. In their grocery stores, they have carcasses of meat hanging in the aisles, and you just go and tell them what you want, and they cut it right there. I mean, there's flies in there and everything and I thought, "Ooo who could even eat the meat from there." But I don't know, I guess they were fine. They used bicycles for everything. I saw a couple riding bikes, moving their mattresses to their new apartment, and it was just kind of a wonderful thing. They had three or four American restaurants that we would go to when we got tired of Chinese. We would go to McDonald's, Kentucky Fried Chicken, and TGI Fridays, and they had a Pizza Hut.

Our hotel was great. I remember they had toilets that were in the ground. In our hotel, they had a Western toilet that was porcelain, but some were holes in the ground, and you had to just squat. Then, you can't put any toilet paper in it, you have to put it in a garbage can instead. It clogs their sewer system, so you can't put it down the hole. I remember I had these overalls that were just lightweight, and I had my camera in the pocket in the front, and when I was in the bathroom there, I almost lost my camera down the hole. I grabbed it just before it went down, and I thought, "Oh my heavens, how terrible I would have clogged their system, and I would have lost all those pictures that I took in China."

We've had a lot of really good, fun trips, and those are just some of the fun times we've had. Our family knows how to have fun when we go places together. We've been on several cruises with them since they've gotten older to different places. We've gone a lot to the Caribbean, and we've been to Hawaii a few times. Those were wonderful trips. We tend to like places that are warm, and they have swimming. We've also had really good times in Mexico and we loved it. The one thing I think about trips is they build the bond between parents and kids because you do a lot of things together. It's not a correction kind of thing, it's a fun kind of thing. So, you build good memories. And that's what we have a lot of.

When we lived in Florida while Brent was in graduate school, we would go to Utah every Christmas for the two weeks. We got off for Christmas break, and in doing so, it was like a 40-hour trip, and we didn't have a lot of money. So, we didn't stay in hotels, and usually, my mom would come up and stay a week or two before and ride back with us in the car. It seems like every time we took this trip, we had a little baby to feed. Back then, the reason we could do it, I guess, is we didn't have all these rules about car seats. So, we had a station wagon when we had all these kids, and they would just make a bed in the very back with a foam mattress. Some of them would sleep back there and some in the seats. They would climb over the seat back and forth for the whole trip.

When we only had Doug and we were moving to Florida, we filled up the back seat with suitcases and then put a board and then put a mattress on there, and we laid him on it. I could just reach around to change him, and we would not even stop the car.. I remember we had no air conditioning, and when we were going through Texas, we just stripped him down to his diaper. It was so darn hot. Whenever I had to change him, I'd have to wipe out all the sand because we'd roll down all the windows so it would be cool enough driving, and the sand would blow in the windows. It would get into all the little crevices of his body, and so I'd have to take a damp cloth and wipe out all of the sand from him. We stayed in a hotel for a couple of days on that trip. One was in New Orleans, and we gave him a good bath.

But as far as the Christmas trip from Florida to Utah, my Mom was usually in there, and we drove straight through. When Brent said he was tired, then I would drive while he would try to sleep. We drove for 40-42 hours, and we traveled non-stop. We would stop at grocery stores to get food and make sandwiches in the car. Once in a while, we'd stop and get treats like ice cream or something like that. But, it was a long trip, and my mom was in the car, so we felt it was hard to stop at a hotel with my mom and get her another room. So that's why we kept traveling until we got there. I cannot say the trip itself was as fun as getting to Utah and seeing all the cousins and the relatives, grandparents and everything. That was the fun part, but the trip was long to get there, and it was a challenge to make sure everybody was having fun and doing good things. We'd stop and let everyone run around in a park or parking lot, go to the bathroom, and then get back in the car and start traveling again.

CHAPTER 9: MEMORIES OF OUR CHILDREN

<u>Mom's Memories of Doug (Audio Vol. 32)</u>

Now, I'll talk a little bit about parenthood, in general – some things we learned, the things I learned,and the process of raising seven kids. At first, I viewed it as a cattle drive with Brent on the left, me on the right, then moving them out. They're all one big group., and we would try to treat them as such, but that didn't work so well. They're individuals. And I learned also that it's more than just individuals, they're individual kids. So that was a big lesson to me. And then I said, as I mentioned, it's not a cattle drive, it's tag team wrestling. Do what you can with one child and then when you can, work with another and let the other go so they can do what they can. As we've mentioned before, there's differences in kids so you can only do so many things together, then you have to treat them separately.

So, we've got some observations. After all the children have grown up and left home, you look back and remember some of the highlights of things you learned.

We can start off with talking about Doug. The main thing I remember about Doug is that he was way into scouting; he earned his Eagle Scout at 14 and set a goal for all the other kids to get them at that same time. But we ended up with a lot of deathbed Eagles right at the last... down in Tallahassee, he put rocks in a neighbor's gas tank, and he would go out and jump up and down on a diving board by our apartment with no fear, but we learned we did some things with the earlier kids that we didn't do with the later kids.

I grew up as an only child, and so I did a lot of babysitting. We had foster kids for a while, but I didn't have a lot of experience as a mother, which I guess nobody does. Doug was very stubborn from the time when he was little. He would really push the limits on everything. For instance, when we lived over in student housing in Florida, Doug was in the process of being potty-trained. If he didn't get his way, he'd have a fit, and I remember he got to the point where he would say no to everything. I would send him to his room, and he would proceed to throw up. He would just throw up! And finally, I realized it was just a battle that no one was winning, and I got smart. Being very calm, I said, "That's fine if you choose to throw up, but I am not going to clean it up. So, if you throw up, you can clean it up." So, he didn't throw up very many times after that because he realized it was not a fun thing to clean up. He would have temper tantrums about different things, and he would do everything he could think of to get his way. When we had a second child, it mellowed Doug out a bit. I always tell this as advice. Even my grandkids, I tell them that when they get married, they should consider at least having two children because I think it really is easier than just having one. It's really good character building because they have to interact with each other.

I remember Doug as our first child, he was manipulating and would make us late for church because he couldn't find his shoes. Brent talked to one of his professors in child development and he said, "That boy is manipulating you. He's telling you what time you're going to church. Let him get ready as much as he can, and then he's got to get in the car." So, we tried that. I would say, "Doug, we're leaving at this time to go to church." I can't remember what he had on, but he didn't have his tie or his shoes on, and so, we went and pulled up to the church. We would go in and sit down near the door to the chapel and all of the sudden, the door to the chapel flew open and he said, "Where is Sue and Brent Barlow?" Then Doug would come walking in with his hair sticking up everywhere, his tie to the side, and carrying his shoes. We did learn from that experience, and gradually, he learned to be on time.

Mom's Memories of Tammy (Audio Vol. 33)

I remember during the teen years that Tammy ran up phone bills like you would not believe. Particularly after her mission because people would call her, and she would always call back, on our phone line. Back then, long distance calls were always pricey. We finally had to take her phone away.

I remember one time, she came and said, "Dad, can I take the car?" I said, "I think it's low on gas." So, she went and filled the gas tank. Then when she got home, she presented her dad with the receipt and told him this was what he owed her.

Another time, she came and said, "Dad, I need money for new underwear. It's so dirty, and it's wearing out." He told her she needed to earn the money for it. She said, "I'm so embarrassed to go out with holy, dirty underwear." So. we advanced her some money. The next day, we found out she went tanning with that money. We were both so mad at her and wondered how we both were taken in on her stories.

Tammy attended BYU Hawaii. She's very friendly. She worked at the PCC as a custodian. When she first got to college there, she was trying to get to know all the kids on her floor at her dorm. She wanted to do something nice so she took the whole floor for pizza and charged the bill on her dad's card. When we got the bill, the reaction was not a pretty sight. Her dad put her on a strict budget with a payback plan after that.

One thing I remember about her was that she would get into more scrapes regarding money. When she lived at home, she would have Kris and Brandon hurry home from school and run through The Orchard to get the mail, so their dad wouldn't see her bills. She had really a lot of issues with managing money.

When she was over in Hawaii, I would call her and say "Tammy, How is your money?" She'd say, "Well, I think it's all right." And I would say, "Well how much do you have?" And she'd say, "Let me call down to the credit union to find out how much I have. She would call me and say I have this amount of money. A couple of days later, she would say I'm in overdraft. She wouldn't account for checks that were already out. After Tammy got married, we were amazed when she went to work in a credit union as a financial advisor. I said that was like putting a fox in with the chickens. I remember that about her. But it was amazing that she did learn to budget her money. After that, she would keep her checkbook accurate down to the penny. I thought "Oh my heavens, this is a miracle." I felt we were never going to make it through with her, or her dad was going to kill her before she made it to her 25th birthday.

While she was working as custodian at the PCC, she became good friends with RobRoy, a fellow worker. RobRoy was planning on going on a mission and invited Tammy to his farewell.

It was at his farewell that Tammy got a feeling that she was supposed to go on a mission. She did go on a mission to Ohio as a result of that feeling. Tammy was very social and well liked. She worried that she didn't know the discussions too well, but I think she converted quite a few people. She also met her future husband there too. He was her Zone Leader and they butted heads a lot. She would always say, "I pity the girl that marries Elder Bevell."

I'm going to recap some of the things from when she was young. I remember when we were living in Wisconsin, and she was taking baton classes. Wisconsin is not the same as Utah in that a lot of their activities are on Sunday. This was always the kind of thing we had to discuss as a family. There were two incidents of her being in a parade and doing her baton thing on Sunday afternoon, and we had a discussion of whether she got to do this or not. There was another incident where she had a little friend who was a little bit different. Nobody liked him at school, and he had a birthday party on Sunday. We talked about it, and we let her go to the birthday party on Sunday because he didn't have any friends. Nobody wanted to come to his birthday party except her. And so that's why we agreed to let her go. On some of the other things in her life, we've told her that we didn't think it was right and that it wasn't keeping the Sabbath Day holy. You have to kind of decide what is the right thing to do and then you have to discuss it, so that they understand that your feelings about keeping the Sabbath Day holy is really important. We were criticized by some members of the church for letting her go. That started a big discussion of who we wanted her to date – a man who was a good Christian or a Latter-day Saint who was kind of flaky.

We had a long discussion, but over the years, we gained confidence in other people, good people in other churches. Tammy was always the kind of person that felt like she had to rescue people. Tammy dated all these guys that had different issues and maybe weren't strong in making wise decisions. They came to church off and on, and it always worried me, but everybody loved her, I mean she could talk to anyone, and she's always been that way, still is today.

Mom's Memories of Brian (Audio Vol. 34)

Next is Brian. We had him in Tallahassee, Florida, and he was healthy after his incident with his hernia that I've already talked about. He was really a good baby, and he just fit in with the other kids. He was always pleasant, and he was kind of funny. He did a lot of fun things at home, and he blended in well. We had a station wagon then, and he would always climb in the back because we didn't have seat belt rules back then like we do now. He would hop in the back, and we had a full mattress back there, so he would go to sleep. He would do that if we had any length of a trip to go on.

One time, he was probably around four or five, and we had to go to a stake conference over in St. Paul, Minnesota from Eau Claire, which took a good while. It was a couple hours anyway to get over there. We had some good friends that we knew from Illinois that moved to St. Paul, the Berrases, and they had a son named Brian who was the same age as our Brian. We went to the stake conference there, and then, they invited us to dinner at their home. After dinner, their Brian and our Brian went out in the backyard. They had a beautiful home with a big, huge yard, all green and lush. The two boys went out there to dig bugs or something out in the dirt, and they were out there forever. It was time for us to head back to Eau Claire, and so, we got everybody in the car settled, and we started going. And then about a part of the way out, one of the kids said, "Where is Brian?" We looked in the back where he usually slept, but there was no Brian. We looked everywhere – under the coats, in the back seat, and everywhere. We realized, "Oh my Heavens, we left Brian?" So, we decided we better go back to St. Paul.

We had to find an exit from the freeway or one that had crossover lanes and make a U turn to go back to St. Paul. And the funny thing about Brian, he didn't even know we were gone. He and the other Brian were still out there playing with bugs and stuff in the backyard. We got there, and we all laughed about it. He wasn't traumatized or whatever, but I think he is one of the kids that we left twice. We left him in another place at the zoo. We stopped at McDonalds on the way back to Grandma Barlow's house, and he had to go to the bathroom. We got up to Brent's parents' home and realized that we didn't have Brian, so we called back to the McDonalds, and they said, "Oh yeah, he's here, he's fine, he's having a hamburger and a malt, and he's doing fine." And so, we went back and got him.

Part of our memories of raising kids is that we left kids three times. We left Brian twice, and we left Jason once. But my comment on that is, I read the scriptures. Joseph and Mary were gone for a day, and they left Jesus behind in the temple. So, we're in good company about not realizing when your kids aren't with you.

Another thing about Brian is that he had a good sense of humor. When Jon was on his mission, he and Jason did a dance to Grease Lightning, and we laughed and laughed. It still is one of my favorites. Brian loved his Grandmother's Day. I think she talked about how she got him interested in wrestling. It's interesting, once he went online for business, he started selling wrestling shirts all over the United States. But people would ask, "What are your kids doing?" And I said, "Well, my son sells products online." And they would say, "Well what does he sell?" And I said, "Wrestling shirts. That kid is a genius. He learned how to do it."

The story about how we left him up at the Salt Lake zoo is controversial. He wrote a paper about how he did it on purpose because he thought he would get some food, and we'd come back and get him. He was a good child though. I think I've told a story about him one night when he and I were home alone. He was downstairs in the basement, and I called him and said on the intercom, "Brian come on up." He said, "No, I'm in bed." I said, "Come up for family prayer." He said, "Just pray over the intercom, and I will listen. I'll kneel down here and pray over the intercom." I got really mad at him, and he came up, but I often wondered if God would answer prayers, even over the intercom, but that's just another memory I have of him.

When Brian was in Jr. High, he went with me to the Drug Store to pick up some items I needed. Brian was in the next aisle looking at stuff. The next thing I knew, two men policeman came down from the upstairs observation room and told Brian they had called the police because they had seen him taking an item and putting it in his pocket. He was being charged with shoplifting. I rushed over to where they were and said, "You must have made some mistake. He is my son and he would never do anything like that." Well, it turned out that he did, and they were going to take him to jail. I talked them into letting him go home with me, saying I would be responsible for him. The next day we had an appointment with the judge. He heard Brian's story and believed him, and sentenced him to Community Service for a few months. It seems Brian had shoplifted because of a dare from his friends. Moral of the story: Be careful of your friends and always listen to your conscience or the Holy Ghost in making choices.

Mom's Memories of Jon (Audio Vol. 35 & 36)

Jon is the middle child. We always think of him as the peacemaker of the family. He is the one that as adults, if something were to happen to my other kids and their kids were left without parents, they would like to have Jon take care of them. He was an all-around good person, he was spiritual, he had good common sense, and he was the one that just kind of mellowed out the family, which we really needed. Sometimes, the ones on either end had some issues at times. But Jon was really good.

One thing I remember about Jon is that he had a really tender heart. When he would ride the bus to school, and I can't remember how old he was, maybe junior high or so, there was an incident on the bus, and the people were teasing this other kid. Jon did participate with them, but their mother came over to our house with that child. Jon was devastated because of what had happened, and he had really just kind of gone along with the group, as kids do. I remember how that affected him and after that you know I think he was more sensitive to others, which is a good learning experience for everyone.

I remember Jon in high school worked at the golf course, and he had an incident probably that still plagues him to this day when he hurt his back lifting golf balls. I remember his dating experiences, and when he was going with certain ones how he felt about it. I remember the most important thing is when he and the Sandy Girls and the Alpine boys would get together and hang out as groups which is where he met Tiff. We're so grateful for that. She went on a mission, and then he went on a mission, but it ended up really well because we're lucky to have her in our family. But Jon was always a really good person. I can't remember anything really terrible about him that happened along the way which is a good thing.

I want to tell you about him sleepwalking. This is when we were living over at 666 North in Orem. He had some friends that lived on the street. We lived on the corner of 1000 E and 666 North, and we had a split-level house. The kids had a double set of bunk beds on the third level, and Jon had started sleepwalking after we had Kris. And so, in the middle of the night one night, I was getting up for a feeding, and all of a sudden, the front door opened and in walked Jon. He didn't have a shirt on, he just had his pajama bottoms. And I said, "Jon, where have you been?" He said, "Oh, I just walked down to Miles' house to see if he could play." And I said, "You realize what time it is," and he said, "No." His eyes were glazed over, and I said, "Well, I think we need to take you down and put you to bed again because it's not time to get up yet." After that, I was really worried that I would not even know where he was in the middle of the night, so I put chairs up and then pots and pans on them so I would hear if he opened the front door. Our bedroom was upstairs, and they were a level down, so I wanted it to make a big noise when he went out. I didn't hear when he went out again one night. He was so good at it, and I never ever heard it. He probably very methodically took all the pans down, unlocked the door, and went out. They did not open their door. It was the middle of the night, and Jon was just perfectly confident. He was barefooted and had no shirt on, and it was cold outside. I don't know at what point in his life he stopped sleepwalking, but I do remember that incident was kind of frightening.

I remember one time we went to get a family picture taken, and Jon was in the back row. Suddenly we heard a crash and looked in the back row. Jon was no longer standing there. I think he locked his legs together and fell over the back. We laughed about it, but it wasn't too funny for him.

I remember Jon also liked to buy old cars to restore them, and he was into fly fishing. I think he's an overall peace maker. Even today, he's still seen as the one who has the confidence from all people in the family, so I think that's a compliment to him. He and Jason are our biggest KSL Classified shoppers because they find more deals there, and they live probably the closest to each other than all the rest of the kids. They have more fun on the things that they buy, and it kind of benefits the whole family because everybody gets into it.

I forgot one important story about Jon, and this was when we were living in Eau Claire, Wisconsin. I was trying to paint the window panes in our bedroom, and I had to scrape the edge off of the glass with a razor blade. Jon wanted me to do something for him, and I was standing on a chair, so he kept pulling my pant leg. I told him to wait, but he kept jerking me. So, the razor blade fell out of my hand and right on the top of his head. It was so scary because his head started spurting blood all over the place. I got some towels and put them on there. Brent taught in Menominee, Wisconsin, which was about a 30-minute drive, so that didn't help. I carried him over with a towel and had my neighbor Mary Fawkner take me to the hospital. They looked at it and said, "Oh Mrs. Barlow. You don't need to worry because the head is one of those areas that bleeds a lot, but it doesn't do any damage because there's a lot of little blood vessels in there." That didn't help me at all. They strapped him down on the bed while they were trying to stop the bleeding. I was in there with him in the room, and he was on the bed screaming, and with all the blood, I found out I was going to faint. And so, they said, "Mrs. Barlow, why don't you wait out in the hall for us?" I was really glad to get out of there because I thought they had it under control, but I wasn't doing anyone any good. It wasn't as serious as I thought, and it healed up really well, but I remember what a frightening experience it was. He did fine, but it was scary at that time. Then, the doctors asked how he got cut. And I said with a razor blade. I then said, "I really am not an abusive mother. It just happened, but still...I will be more careful."

Mom's Memories of Jason (Audio Vol. 37)

I remember several things about Jason. I think she talked about his birth, the leboyer method, and him being kind of mild-mannered because of that birth. One of the other things that stands out about Jason is when he got left down at Hamburger World, and we don't know how that happened. I think Kris went back in to get him, and she came back, and we thought Jason was with her, but the embarrassing thing about that was we didn't know we'd left him. We went out, and the cops brought him home in a cop car and wanted to know why Dr. Brent Barlow, who had taught marriage and family at BYU, had left his kid. He was grateful for that ride. But again, three times we've left kids. Well, Jason had a great time. They came in with a big milk shake. They gave him anything he wanted there, and he got to ride in a cop car. We had gone to Jim and Robins, our neighbors, and were in their backyard when we realized we didn't have Jason. He was in the cop car at the time we called their house, and so we had a hard time tracking him down, so we just met the cop at our house and that's how we got him.

The other thing I remember about Jason's birth when we were in Eau Claire is that Sue had to have her thyroid taken care of, but the other members of the church would come over and sit with her all night. We learned the hospitality of people.

I'll talk a little bit about the birth of Jason after the laboyer thing. This lady that lived in Menominee had seven kids and a newborn. It was about 30 miles away where I gave birth to Jason, but she came over to the hospital. I didn't even know about this. She had nursed her baby and put her to sleep, and then, she drove 30 miles over to the hospital. And I said, "What are you doing here? You have a family." And she said, "No, in our family, it's a policy that they always have to have a family member stay over the first night after surgery."

So, she sat there. She brought some crocheting to do. And all night long, I would just wake up a little, and we would talk for a while, and then, I would go back to sleep. She stayed there all night long, and we had the nicest conversations. The next morning, at about 7 AM, she got her things altogether and she said, "I think I better go back because my baby will be hungry." And so, she drove back to Menominee, but I always have a soft spot even now for her and for the selflessness that she had in thinking about me at that time. We didn't even know each other that well. They came to church and had to drive 30 miles away, but really it created a bond between us that I will never ever forget.

I have to tell a story about ministering or visiting and teaching that comes to mind as what it means to give yourself in a way that's not always easy, so that you can help another person. Just a side note too, I learned some things having grown up in and being around LDS all my life. I was apprehensive about going away from Utah and interacting with people who are not LDS. And I remember once you had Tammy, one of my good friends who was just a good Christian man, went down to the hospital to visit. He didn't have to, but I was always impressed with his thoughtfulness. And then, when I taught at University Wisconsin Stout, Frank Backus was a good friend, and he was a Methodist Minister, so I learned that through those experiences that there are good people in other churches as well.

Next, we will talk about Kris.

I have memories I wrote about in my Deseret News column. I wrote one column about Kris. She was very outgoing with her prayers. I remember one time she prayed that she would spit on her brothers. She learned that she was going to pray in a very spiritual way. The other thing we remember most about Kris is when she got the pen stuck up her nose, which is one of the big memories.

I was up at BYU and Sue was supposed to come and pick me up, and I didn't know where she was. I called home. Jon answered the phone in his John Wayne voice. I asked, "How are things, Jon?" He said, "They're fine, Dad. Did you hear about the accident?" I said, "No." He said, "Kris got a pen stuck up her nose. We tried to get a hold of you and mom. We didn't know how to get you. So, we called the home teachers, brother Orton and brother Keiffer, and they came and took her down to the hospital. I think she still has the x-ray of that pen stuck up her nose. But that was an unusual experience about why she did it.

Other things I remember about Kris is when she worked in high school at a home care center where she learned to care for aging people. She created a sensitivity for it.

I remember when Kris was in high school her very best friend Ashley got killed in an automobile accident, and it was a sad thing. Kris spoke at her funeral. She had many memories of her. Kris' daughter Layla has her middle name after Ashley, and Layla knows where her middle name comes from. It just shows you how friends can influence us, even as we grow up.

Kris worked at Abercrombie in Hawaii when she was over there going to school. She was also a waitress. She quit Abercrombie because they wanted her to wear a swimsuit that was kind of revealing. And they wanted her to be part of a photo shoot, and she didn't feel that was good, so she quit Abercrombie. She worked at the Mexican restaurant, and she was really good with people, even though they were drunk. One time, she got a tip for $100 while working there. Kristen also was one, like Tammy, that would try to help people. She was a big helper, and I remember she went with a guy named Scott in high school, and in fact, she helped Scott at one time, you know, he had been on drugs and drinking and whatever at one time in his life, but he was on the mend a bit when he started dating Kristen. And she really was a good influence on him, and he went on a mission. I think he really thought he was going to marry her when he got home, but he got home, and it just wasn't the same. Part of the reason was Kris always wanted to wear heels and stuff, and she wanted someone who was taller, which is a silly reason. But, she and Scott are still good friends. Scott came over to see them when she and Jeremy were living over in Hawaii, and he came over and stayed with Jeremy and Kris.

One of the big things I remember about Kris is that she always wanted to go on a mission. She wanted to go for a semester or two and then go on a mission. She got over there, met Jeremy, fell in love, and he proposed to her. She called me on the phone, "Oh Daddy, What would I do about my mission? I'm in love with Jeremy." I gave her a quote from Bruce R McConkie, "The most important thing you do in your life is to marry the right person in the right place by the right authority." And then I said, "After you get married, Kris, you can be a missionary to your family, to your spouse." I look where they went, where they've been to Costa Rica, and they were missionaries. And so, she has been a missionary. So, we learned from that experience that if you don't go out at the time you expected, you could be a missionary at another time. So, she's done a lot of good that way, but I always remember that, how she agonized over that decision. But, she and Jeremy worked it out and got married. They were going to get married in August, and then they postponed it. The wedding announcements were already out, and so we had to send a postcard saying it was postponed until later. I had mixed feelings because she told me she couldn't talk to me. She thought I'd be too emotional over the issue, so she would talk to dad all the time.

Jeremy was wonderful because he came down and went to UVU so he could be closer to Kris, and they could date and work through their things and still get married later. We loaned him the red fury truck, and he would drive that back and forth from our house to date Kris during that time. He's such a great guy, and he's so kind. It was a good match for her to marry Jeremy, and he's such a good father and husband that he just added a lot, and he's so always complimentary. One thing about Jeremy which I know this isn't about him, but he is one of the very first to wish everybody happy birthday in our family, so he's very, very thoughtful, and Kris made a good choice in marrying him.

Mom's Memories of Brandon

After one year old, Brandon became a lot more mobile. His casts were removed for good and he could go more places and get into more trouble. Since Brandon was the last kid in our family, he was spaced so that he wasn't in the same schools as his brothers and sisters. Therefore, he got away with a lot of things that I would have normally caught. Two main things that I know Brandon excels in is Computer Skills and working with people. Brandon is so smart in figuring things out. In fact, if it has anything to do with cell phones or computers, Brandon's the go-to-guy. Brandon has great patience with youth, not only his own kids, but kids who have been in trouble or have behavior skills with authority figures. I remember him working with special needs youth at Timpanogos High School, and he had them doing amazing things. Brandon is very good at teaching others. He is able to explain new concepts in simple terms so a person with little or no skills can comprehend. He is well sought after and has excelled in working for various companies and has gotten several leadership awards.

As far as jobs growing up, Brandon delivered autoparts at one job and delivered diamonds to a Salt Lake store. He also worked at Springville Boys Ranch where he worked with troubled youth as a counselor. In fact, he met his wife there one summer when they worked together.

One funny (for me) incident when Brandon was in high school, one of his siblings saw his car in a church parking lot on their way home from school. She recognized his car, and so we tracked him down. He was making out in the back of his car. He was so embarrassed!

Brandon has a high tolerance for pain. When he was in Jr. High, he came to me saying he had a stomach ache. It didn't go away, so I took him to the doctor to make sure it wasn't serious. It is good that I did because his appendix had ruptured, so they had to take him in for surgery ASAP and clean it all up. I had no idea. He had to stay in the hospital for 10 days to fight the infection.

The other incident I remember was when he was working in Springville at the Boys' Ranch. He had found out that Kaitie was getting him a motorcycle for his upcoming birthday, and he didn't know how to ride a motorcycle. This friend of his told him he would teach him to ride after work in the parking lot. Well, Brandon did get on the motorcycle and was riding around the parking lot. He was taking a turn too fast, and slid in some gravel and fell to the side on his leg and ankle. The bike was heavy and did some damage to his leg. Brandon didn't know if he had insurance that would cover the ambulance cost to Payson Hospital so his friend drove him over in his car. The bone was sticking out of his leg and there was a lot of blood. I can't imagine how much pain he was in when they were riding in the car to the hospital. And they had to transfer him again up to the Provo Hospital.

Brandon was and is a jokester. He always tells me he wants a Tesla for his birthday. But I know I can go to Brandon with any problem. He has always been there for me. I know he loves Kaitie and all of his kids and is a caring person.

CHAPTER 10: POST COLLEGE, RETIREMENT AND MISSION

Sue and Brent's Memories from their CES Mission in Duluth
Stake, Minnesota (Audio Vol. 50)

Sue: On this subject, we're going to talk together about our CES Mission to Minnesota, Minneapolis.

Brent: 2009 to 2010.

Sue: Right. We went for a year, and we were assigned to the Duluth, Minnesota, area, which is the largest area mission in the United States. It goes into Southern Canada at Thunder Bay, which we traveled a lot. It's a traveling kind of mission. You go and stay overnight in a motel in faraway places, and it's kind of a fun mission because it almost feels like a vacation when you get to see little things about different cities. But also, the people that live far away, they really are active in seminary and institutes. They really have a love for it, and they don't get a lot of people that come out there for the church because they're away from the hub of the church, and they don't get as many experiences. So, they really love for you to visit and are really interested in your input. (New Pic 47)

Brent: As Sue said, it was the largest geographical mission in the church, and the Stake President, how far away did he live? He'd ride his motorcycle down to the chapel, and it was…

Sue: Well, he kind of lived in our area, but sometimes he would travel. He had a motorcycle and traveled everywhere. He would travel down to Central Minnesota for meetings, or his counselors would travel up there and meet once a week. It was a several hour thing – it wasn't just a 10-minute deal. So, they were dedicated. I mean, there's not many people that are more dedicated than they were. They really did a service to the church.

Brent: And I remember too, we found out that not too long before, there were members up at Thunder Bay in Canada that used to have to drive down to Duluth, which is 100 miles plus, for church. They determined it was too far for them to drive 100 miles, so they told them to just come every other Sunday. We look back, and all the churches in our area were just within a few blocks of where we lived. But there's people driving 100 miles to attend church meetings. We were impressed with the seminary teachers, mothers and fathers sometimes, who would drive great distances for early morning seminary, and their kids would have to be there at the meetings at 6 o'clock. The parents would drive them 30 miles, wait for them, and drive them back. But that impressed us – how much the parents were committed to get their kids to early morning seminary.

Brent and I as Senior Missionaries

Sue: Let me talk a little bit about going to Thunder Bay. The road travels along the edge of Lake Superior, and it's cold. Lake Superior is a really cold lake, first of all. Wisconsin and Minnesota have really cold winters, and the roads are icy sometimes going up to Thunder Bay in the wintertime. And they have a lot of animals. We've seen moose, bears, and all sorts of other animals cross those roads. It's especially dangerous in the evening. They said, "Watch and drive carefully." Because deer will cross the road, all kinds of things cross the road, and if you're not careful, you'll hit one, especially when the roads are icy, and you can't stop. So, it's kind of scary for them to have to do that, even though they're probably more used to it than we were. But, to illustrate this, we lived in an apartment that was right next to the Stake Center, and in the wintertime, we would drive over there, even though it was next door, because it was so icy out. When we drove over there, even getting out of the car to go into the church, if you didn't put your gloves on or a scarf over your nose, your nose would freeze together. And the other thing I remember about Minnesota and Wisconsin, where we used to live, is the snow. Once they plow the first snowstorm, the snow never goes away because it stays cold, so they just keep piling it on top. All of the fire hydrants have these extensions – this long, brightly colored kind of a rod – so that if you're coming to a corner, you can see over the snow drifts. When they plow the snow onto the side of the roads, it makes it high on the corners. So, when you're pulling up there in your car, you don't always see another car coming from either side. So that's why they put them there. And also, it's for the firemen, so if there is a fire, they can see where the fire hydrants are.

Brent: But, we were impressed too. They were used to dealing with the snow. The bulldozers would be out early, but what Sue is saying too is that the snow drifts were so high along the road, sometimes we'd be pulling up to a four-way stop, and you'd see this little ball going along. It was the Volkswagens. They had to have the thing high enough, so you would know there was a car coming. It was cold, but they knew how to take care of the roads there. Just a side note, when we lived there and it would snow, I'd say, "Well, I'll just wait for a couple of hours to go out and shovel the walks." By the time I got to it, the snow would have turned to ice. My neighbors taught me, "Brent, you need to get out there as soon as it's through snowing, when it's still soft." And so, I learned you don't wait to do it, you just get it off while you can.

Sue: One thing about living in Utah, some people take their shoes off when they go into their house – it's more of a thing now than it used to be when I was growing up. But in Minnesota and Wisconsin, everybody really honors that code, especially in the winter, because if not, you track in all that stuff from outside. So, you better have easy removal of your boots because they have them right by their door or out on their front porch to keep their house clean.

Brent: I want to digress back to another topic. We learned the importance of early morning seminary, particularly for those high school students whose parents were not active in the church or didn't believe in it. They would come, and the seminary teachers were so dedicated because they'd have to get up early and travel sometimes. But, we learned how important it was that these young people had access to people outside of the home. I took from that, that even when you get back here, where the churches are larger, other adults can really have an impact on your children. Some of these kids came to seminary when their parents didn't even go to church, but the seminary teachers were still able to get through to some of them.

Sue: We had a couple of seminaries with students who lived quite a ways away, around 20-30 miles, so we would Skype. And that's the first time I've ever been to a seminary that Skypes with people. It was really cool because the person that was on the other line participated as if she were there in person. Sometimes she'd say the prayer, sometimes she'd have comments about certain Scriptures, or sometimes she would take a turn reading Scriptures. So, they just knew they had to get up and log in early in the morning for seminary. And that way, we could reach a lot more people than we could if it was impossible for them to get there for seminary early in the morning.

Brent: And the controversy became, "Can they learn as much on Skype as they can in person?" But now, it's quite obvious. In the church, young people can learn either way. One other major event happened to me when I was back in Eau Claire. The church was usually pretty good about clearing the driveways, but we were over there one day for something, and someone couldn't back their car out of the driveway. Some of us went out, being the good people we were, and we were trying to pull the car back. Somehow, I fell back on my head. It knocked me out. Everybody was so concerned, but it was just for a few minutes. I can still remember the ringing in my ears. I had to go to the doctors to see if I had any concussions. That was January 29th, 2010. I had gone to the doctor and tried different medications, but I was just low on energy from that experience. Sue ended up doing a lot of the record keeping while I recovered. But that was kind of a scary experience. Should we talk about Carlton Branch now?

Sue: Okay, one thing, and this has to do with Carlton branch as well. But one thing about the church making changes in the local area so that more people could attend their meetings, they would have their meetings at the Stake Center once a month. We would have all organizations at the church. We would do the seminary institutes there, and people would travel from wherever they were to be there. We'd have a lunch provided at the Stake level, and then, they would travel back. They would leave by 3 o'clock, so that they would be back before it got too dark. And this was really fun because it became a big social event as well. People enjoyed it because in the mission field, they only know the people in their wards or branches. So, they really, especially the youth, look forward so much to being able to get together with other youth. This once-a-month thing, it was really beneficial to them. They would have Scripture Bowls and all these different kinds of things for the youth. Things like this kept a lot of people in the church. So, that was really a huge benefit for their area.

Brent: We learned the importance of the social aspect of the church, and I thought of Maslow's hierarchy of needs. People have physical, social, mental, and spiritual needs. The physical is that you need to be fed and healthy. But then the social… I think we underestimate the fellowship – that's where a lot of these young people would come to Saturday meetings that had the social aspect of the Gospel and build rapport with not only other adults, but other teachers. All in all, when we got back up from the mission, we just thought how blessed we were here to have a chapel so close. They traveled once a month to St Paul Temple.

Sue: Okay, so now, Carlton Branch used to be a ward. There was a big industrial factory there, and I can't remember what they made, but a lot of the people that work there were LDS and had come from other areas. The area for the church was quite large, so they built a chapel there, which is very unusual for a branch to have a chapel. And so, it was stage two. When they build churches out there, they don't build the whole thing. They build the chapel and a bigger area for when they have social events. It has a portable set up so they can take away the chairs and everything, and it becomes a recreational hall. It's kind of an all-purpose thing. Theirs was stage two, so it had a kitchen and a few classrooms in it. It was very versatile. And one thing about Carlton Branch, because of the distance so many people had to travel, it was a two-hour meeting instead of the usual three-hour meeting. It was kind of like we do now. However, theirs was, we would meet at the beginning of… And we would attend either primary or Relief Society priesthood and Sunday school. It was kind of a combined thing. Now, Primary was kind of interesting. I was the first counselor in the Primary, and the Branch president's wife was the president. We were always prepared for Primary, but there were times when no one would show up. We would go there, and no kids would come, so then, we would just go into Relief Society. But, I noticed there was such a diversity of knowledge. I remember I was teaching about Christmas, the nativity, and the Savior's birth, and some of the kids had never even heard the story of Christmas. I thought everybody in the world knew the story of the Savior's birth. But we acted it out, and we did all these things for it. I just thought everyone knew the Gospel, but they didn't. So, we came back to square one and started very simply and built upon that. They really liked it, and they would come. Sometimes, they were the only ones that came to church in their family. They either came with a neighbor or a friend, or some relative that was a member of the church, who came and wanted to bring them along. So, it was really a missionary experience as we did that. And they had a lot of socials and potlucks there. When there was a baptism or after Fast Sunday, we would have a big potluck. There were Linger Longers, and everybody had their own signature food they brought every month. There was one guy there who always brought the potato salad because he made the best potato salad ever. There were certain different things that everybody would bring, and it was always wonderful, so everybody looked forward to it. On those Sundays, more people would come to church just because of the food.

Brent: And I remember too how small our branch was. We didn't have any teenagers. We had one young man, whose hair hung down to his shoulders, and he was the one to pass the sacrament with the help of some other elders. But I wondered if I'd been judgmental, "Should we let that kid pass the sacrament with his hair down to his shoulders?" But they thought, "Well, he's the only one we got, so try to keep him in." But that was a different kind of branch. It was a small branch with two-hour meetings, and we traveled about 20 miles.

Sue: This guy that did the sacrament, he wore cowboy boots and jeans, but he had a white shirt on. And really, the family was very loving, and they were very spiritual, and they did more things in their family than other families were doing, like studying the scriptures and listening to general authorities talks.

Brent: And we tried not to be too judgmental of his dress after that because they were associated with the church.

Sue: They were good people, yeah. And the whole ward was like that, they were just very accommodating, and they were very welcoming, so it was really nice to go to a place like that, where everybody welcomed you in.

CHAPTER 11: OTHER FAMILY STORIES

The Brass Bucket (Audio Vol. 21)

I want to mention the story of the brass bucket. We have this bucket that came across the plains with my great-grandmother, my mom's grandma. It is a brass bucket, and it even has a hole in it. It's well-worn because they used to carry wood in it or do other things with it. It's all really tarnished and everything because it's so old. Unless you're a collector of those things, it's not anything wonderful to look at. My mom loved it, and because of its history, she really wanted somebody in her family to have it, and so she told me that this bucket was mine, and I should take it. So, I had it over at my house, and sometimes, I'd put weeds in it, put it by the fireplace, or different things like that. I knew how much my Aunt Mary loved this bucket. And so, I thought after my mom passed away, I would give her the bucket because it meant a lot to her.

My mom raised her since she was a baby, so she looked at my mom as her own mom as well because her mom died when she was just a baby. I had planned on giving this bucket to her. One day, she came over to my house and asked me if I still had the brass bucket. We got to talking and everything, and she went on to say that she felt this brass bucket needed to go to someone in the family from the blood line. She didn't think it should go to me because I was adopted. All of the feelings that I ever had about that brass bucket going to her vanished, and I told her that I was just as much a part of the family as she was because I was sealed to my parents, so I felt that I would like to keep the bucket and pass it on to my children.

She thought I was wrong, and that it should go to a bloodline member of the family. I said, "Well that's your opinion, but I'm sorry, I feel that it should go to one of my kids." And so that was the story of the bucket. In thinking about how important it is that you're a member of the family, it doesn't matter if you're adopted, as long as you're born under the covenant, you are the same in the Lord's eyes. So that's the story of the bucket.

Spiritual Experiences with my Family (Audio Vol. 40)

Have you ever had a supernatural experience or an experience you couldn't explain? Before my grandpa died, my grandpa Jacklin had a stroke along with several mini strokes. As he wasn't making much progress in the hospital, it was decided to take him over to Lehi to my Aunt Metz's house and they put a hospital bed up in the kitchen, so he could look out the kitchen window. Also, the kitchen is a place where people like to gather, and grandpa always liked to be around people.

Well, a few days went by, then he passed away in the night. I can remember what happened because this incident happened about a couple of nights after my grandpa passed. I didn't witness this, but my mother told me the next morning that she went to get a drink of water. She turned around, and my grandpa was sitting in the chair in the kitchen, and he said, "Alice, could you get me a drink of water?" So, she turned around to get another glass with a drink of water for him, and he was gone. My mom, in retelling the incident, just says, "This was his way of saying that he was okay, that he was fine, and they didn't need to mourn for him or anything."

There's a lot of stories in the Jacklin Family about different people that visited relatives on the earth. My Uncle Jesse had one experience right before he died. People from the other side of the veil visited him and told him they needed their temple work done. You have to realize that my Uncle Jesse was not a stalwart member of the church; in fact, the only time he went to church was maybe if one of the kids got baptized. He smoked all the time, and he would drink and sit at the table in front of the kitchen window with only his jockey shorts on, smoking a cigarette and drinking a beer. That's the picture I have of my Uncle Jesse, and I really didn't like him that much, but I thought well, if people on the other side of the veil could visit my Uncle Jesse they must really, really need their work done because my Uncle Jesse would be the last person I would go to. Afterwards, he told the family about his experience, and they looked up the individuals and found out that they were relatives, and the work got done.

I remember when I learned about the Joseph Smith story. In the early years of the church, people would get visitations from angels and people from the other side who would either come to restore something to the earth or bring a special message from the other side. And so, we have all those stories that are so important. It kind of freaked me out, and so when I would pray at night, I would say my prayers with a light on. I didn't want to offend anyone, but I would ask people that were on the other side of the veil to please stay there and not visit me because it would freak me out.

Now that I'm older, I think it would be a very peaceful thing, but when I was little, it would just make me nervous. But if you read about other incidents, when people on the other side visited someone here, it was either a comforting experience or it was something that would help them change their lives.

CHAPTER 12: CONCLUSION

Dear Family,

This has been a great experience for me; the memories I have, and the experiences I've had with Brent and our 7 kids. I am so blessed to have this honor of being the mother to such a nice group of kids or adults as they are now. Everyone has special gifts they bring to this family.

And they all have a certain sensitivity to each other that is priceless. I hope that when you read this, that you will laugh, cry, and remember the fun times we have had together and hope that we will still have many years left to make more memories.

This last picture is one of our family in its young stages. Think of all the things that have happened since that picture was taken. We are so lucky that we still have a bond together and that we all are moving forward. Even this book hasn't taken me to where I am today. Since the Orem houses we have lived in, we've lived in South Jordan in two different places, the one in Garden Park at 11022 South Fennell Way, and where we live now, at South Jordan View, at 11352 South Redwood Road, Unit 341. Both places have good memories already with many more to be made.

Life is good as long as it keeps moving us along. I want to tell all of you that I am so proud of all of you and what you are making of your life. When I hold little Iris, our latest grandchild in my arms, she helps me to remember when you, my children, were just that size and I would look at your little fingers and toes and those searching eyes of wonderment and realize how blessed I was to have that experience of having you in my life.

How lucky I am to have a life with Brent. Together we started this family for which I am extremely proud, happy, grateful and blessed. I love you all so much. We are all so blessed to have a family such as ours!

Love From,
Sue
Mom
Grandma
Great Grandma

34658f27-ed6a-49fc-830b-413c23a1c22aR01